LOST IN
LOST IN SPACE.

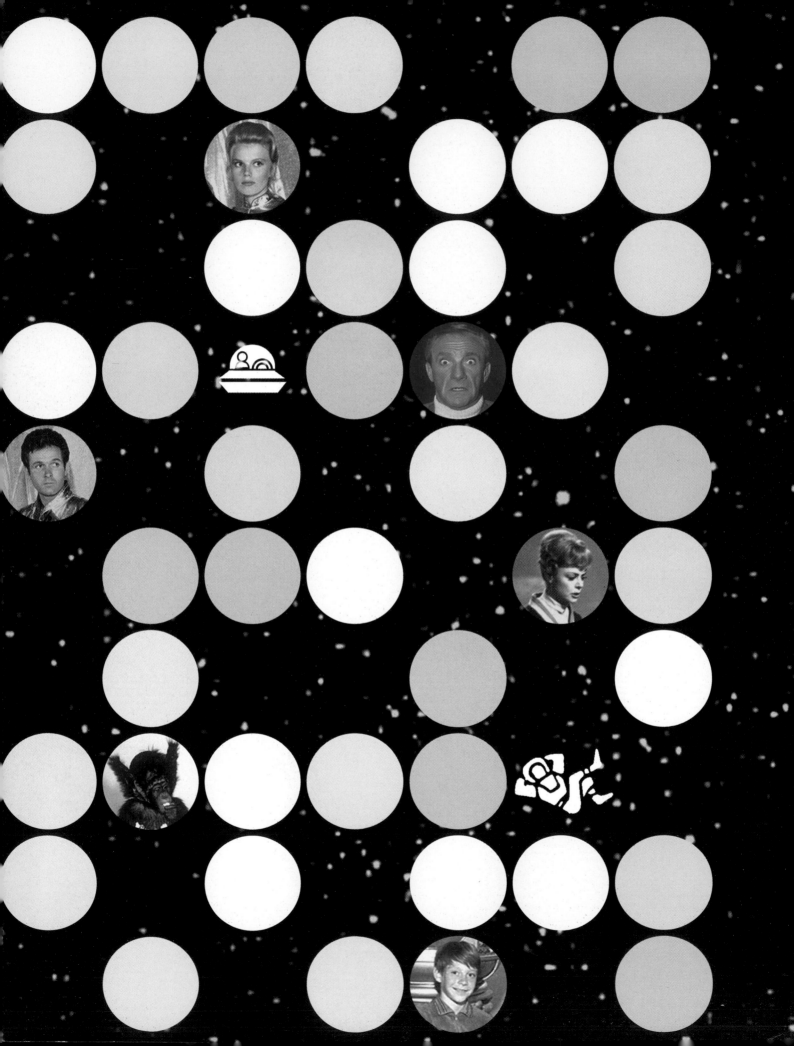

LOST IN
LOST IN SPACE

Pop Culture and Space Adventure with the Space-Traveling Robinsons

MARK COTTA VAZ

HarperPrism
A Division of HarperCollinsPublishers

To the memory of Irwin Allen, a true ringmaster of thrills;
to the talented producers, casts, and crews who created
Lost in Space *for TV and the movies; and to my father,*
August—himself an explorer of space and time

CONTENTS

ACKNOWLEDGMENTS

A special appreciation to John Silbersack at HarperPrism (John, this comes full circle from *Spirit*!) . . . My thanks to editor John Douglas, who was Alpha Control to my *Jupiter 2*, but always in contact with sage advice, direction, and assistance . . . My appreciation to Rich Miller for his stellar assistance from the HarperPrism side . . . Thanks to Bruce and Ginny Walters for the assistance of XO Digital Arts throughout (including work on the author's time-traveling photo) . . . And a big, Buck Rogers–sized thank-you to Bob Burns, who was helpful above and beyond the call (you *are* Two-Dollar Rogers!) . . . Cheers and salutations to my agent, Victoria Shoemaker, an advocate for books and the magic of the written word.

A tip of the old *chapeau* to Jim Eiden for providing me with tapes of the original *Lost in Space* TV broadcasts—kudos as well to Sue Eiden and their children, Emily and Michael—and to Steve ("Oh, the pain!") and Annie Eiden, for sharing the experience (and here's to the brood, Kristen and Jennifer) . . . John Smith was a stand-up guy on the New Line side, while Scott Hartford was most helpful at Foxstar Productions . . . And to Don Shay, Steve Staples, and Terry Jones: "Thanks for the leads!" . . . Carlos Fontanot and other media contacts at the Johnson Space Center in Houston, Texas, were superb in their swift response to a request for images—the out-of-this-world NASA images herein are thanks to their efforts . . . Thanks as well to Brigitte J. Keuppers, librarian and archivist at the UCLA Arts Library–Special Collections, for facilitating access to archival material dedicated to Irwin Allen (thanks also to Irwin's widow, Sheila Allen, for granting it).

Despite being in ill health, veteran *Lost in Space* concept artist Tom Cranham contributed his thoughts with insight and good humor. Tom passed away on November 19, 1997. Our condolences to his family, friends, and colleagues.

General hugs and high-five's all around to my godchildren Johnny and Alexandra and to future space travelers Daniel, Matt, Michael, Kate, and Joey . . . *Muito obrigado* to my dad (whose voluminous library provided some of my reference materials), my mother (for life on the spiritual plane), and my sisters and brothers: Katherine, Maria, Patrick, Peter, and Teresa . . . And (as always) a kiss for Olga and a hug for Liza.

I would have been lost in space if not for the following interview subjects, whose insights have enlivened this book: Roy Alexander, Eric Brevig, Len Brown, Bob Burns, Kevin Burns, Vince Calandra, Tom Cranham, Charles Csuri, Jim Danforth, Merrill Dean, Roger Gilbertson, Ned Gorman, Bill Griffith, Terry Jones, Rick McCallum, Todd McFarlene, Ralph McQuarrie, Dr. Edgar Mitchell, Mark Moore, Joe Musso, Dr. Frank Norick, Mark Setrakian, and Stan Winston. I *did* get lost in space when I hooked up with most of the original TV cast members who graciously shared their thoughts: Jonathan Harris, Marta Kristen, June Lockhart, Bob May, Bill Mumy, and Dick Tufeld.

*Mythologies are huge cairns of anything and everything
that helps to explain a people to itself.*

—ROBERTSON DAVIES, THE MERRY HEART, 1996

*Today, space travel is one of the ultimate goals of scientific and military research. The
familiar cry, "Who rules the moon controls the earth!" reflects our readiness to exploit
space. Our military might is ready for space; our economic strength is ready for space;
soon our ships will be ready for space.*

—ALBRO T. GAUL, THE COMPLETE BOOK OF SPACE TRAVEL, 1956

*As of this moment, 1800 hours October 21, 1997, all efforts to restore communication
with Jupiter 2 and America's first space family have been unsuccessful. . . .
It is now believed that the tragic fate of the Jupiter 2 and its occupants may be the
result of sabotage by an agent of foreign powers.*

—NAMELESS PUBLIC RELATIONS SPOKESMAN SPEAKING BEFORE A TELEVISION CAMERA
AT ALPHA CONTROL, CAPE KENNEDY, IN "THE DERELICT,"
LOST IN SPACE EPISODE TWO, SEASON ONE, 1965

TO THE STARS !

CLASSICS Illustrated

Special Issue

35c

In December of 1961, when Classics Illustrated published this special "To the Stars!" issue, the "Space Race" was on: Soviet cosmonaut Yuri Gagarin had completed the first manned orbital flight, Alan Shepard's Freedom 7 suborbital flight made him the first American in space, and Gherman S. Titov rode the Vostok 2 into the history books with the first long-duration flight.

INTRODUCTION

October 21, in the Earth year of Nineteen Hundred and Ninety-seven; somewhere in space. We've come to the end of the first 24 hours of the voyage and all are in good health. As yet we have no inkling of our true position. The period during which we traveled hyperdrive beyond the speed of light could have carried us through space and time to almost any part of the galaxy. . . .

Now, as Major West continues to search for some clue to our present location, there's little for any of us to do but rest and wait and hope.

—PROFESSOR JOHN ROBINSON, COMMANDER OF THE JUPITER 2, SHIP'S LOG ENTRY, IN "THE DERELICT," LOST IN SPACE EPISODE TWO, SEASON ONE

It was *the* news item of 1997: Earth's pioneering first family in space, the advance guard and best hope for an overpopulated planet, was bound for possibly habitable worlds in Alpha Centauri when things went horribly wrong. The U.S. Alpha Control space mission headquarters on Earth had lost contact with the all-American *Jupiter 2* crew and sadly concluded the worst. Presumed dead were astrophysicist Professor John Robinson, his biochemist wife, Maureen, their children, Judy, Penny, and Will, and Major Don West.

Alpha Control had been correct in its suspicions that an agent of foreign powers had sabotaged America's mission to colonize the stars. What ground control didn't know was that the crew was still alive, having landed their crippled spacecraft on a desolate, seemingly lifeless planet with the mysterious saboteur Dr. Zachary Smith trapped aboard.

Thankfully, the space castaways found themselves on a habitable world of breathable air, arable soil, and drinkable water. But it was also a place of

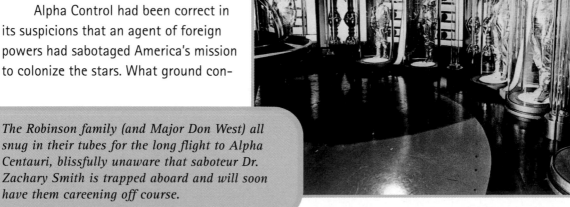

The Robinson family (and Major Don West) all snug in their tubes for the long flight to Alpha Centauri, blissfully unaware that saboteur Dr. Zachary Smith is trapped aboard and will soon have them careening off course.

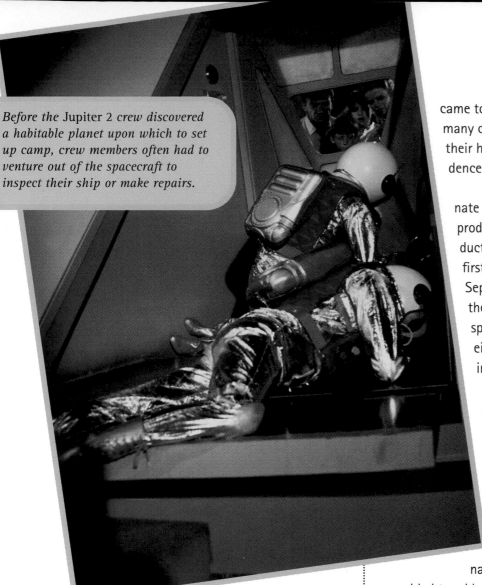

Before the Jupiter 2 *crew discovered a habitable planet upon which to set up camp, crew members often had to venture out of the spacecraft to inspect their ship or make repairs.*

came to the lonely shores of America so many centuries ago, and who found it in their hearts to give thanks to providence for their blessings."

This drama unfolded in an alternate 1997, a future dreamed up by producer Irwin Allen and his TV production team. *Lost in Space*, which first aired on the CBS network on September 15, 1965, would feature the triumphs and travails of the space-traveling Robinsons through eighty-three episodes extending into the 1968 season.

On June 25 of the *real* 1997 a space disaster would indeed capture the attention of the world, as a remote-controlled robot cargo ship crashed into the orbiting Russian *Mir* space station during a docking maneuver. The three-man crew, two Russian cosmonauts and an American astronaut, scrambled to address the life-threatening damage. And then Russian commander Vasily Tsibliyev pulled the wrong plug on an onboard computer, sending the space station into a spin, cutting the power, and plunging *Mir* into dark and cold.

Meanwhile, the National Aeronautics and Space Administration (NASA) enjoyed the triumph of the orbiting space shuttle *Columbia*, which successfully completed a sixteen-day mission of science experiments. And on July 4 the Mars Pathfinder mission set down on Mars—the first unmanned American craft to do so since the 1976 *Viking* mission—transmitting back to Earth haunting photographs of a desolate Martian flood plain. Most remarkable of all, Pathfinder's two-foot-long *Sojourner* robot rover was able to move via remote control signals sent across 119 million miles of

deserts and rugged mountain ranges, with weather conditions fluctuating between extremes of blistering heat and freezing cold. And who knew what dangers lay out there in the darkness of night, beyond the perimeter of the spacecraft's protective force field? Meanwhile, inside the damaged ship itself lurked Dr. Smith, who had gained control of the ship's onboard environmental control robot and seemed to be biding his time before he would destroy them all.

But John Robinson, a scientist dedicated to God, family, and country, would face the unknown future with courage in his heart and fire in his eyes. As he would write in his commander's log: "All of us feel somehow akin to those hardy souls who first

space from NASA's Jet Propulsion Laboratory in Pasadena, California. From there controllers wearing stereoscopic goggles worked a 3-D mouse while viewing a monitor that translated transmitted images into the three-dimensional form vital for accurate remote-control navigation on the Martian surface. Several months later, NASA's *Global Surveyor* would successfully be put into Martian orbit and begin its task of mapping the Red Planet from above.

Orbiting stations and space shuttles, robots and satellites on Mars, even the dramatic (and ultimately successful) effort to maintain the *Mir* space station—such wonders were once the stuff of science fiction. But while the imaginary 1997 conjured up for *Lost in Space* did not anticipate such breakthroughs as personal computers and the Internet (back then computer technology was represented by

huge, monolithic mainframes), the Robinsons were far ahead of us in space travel technology. In fact, John Robinson himself would be mightily dismayed at what slackers we've been in the space-traveling department. Considering the Space Age dreams of the fifties and sixties, he would have assumed that by now there'd be space colonies on the moon and *manned* missions to Mars.

More than a relic of an earlier TV era or mere grist for global syndica-

(TOP RIGHT) Mir, *moments after its undocking from the space shuttle* Atlantis *on November 18, 1995.* (RIGHT) *The* Mir *space station, as seen from the space shuttle* Atlantis *during docking approach on January 14, 1997.*
(ABOVE) *On November 25, 1997, newspapers published this image of spacewalking* Columbia *shuttle astronauts preparing to make a daring recovery of the errant* Spartan *astronomy satellite. While secured to opposite ends of the shuttle's cargo bay, Japanese astronaut Takao Doi* (RIGHT) *and American astronaut Winston Scott waited for the satellite's telescopic tube ends to rotate into position so they could grab and, with the aid of a robot arm, safely stow the* Spartan *into the cargo bay. (Photos courtesy of NASA.)*

THE UNITED STATES AIR FORCE PRESENTS:

The "HIDDEN CREW"

The prototypical American astronaut was found in the military: The first seven astronauts selected for the pioneering man-in-space Project Mercury *program were all military jet test pilots.*

The Hidden Crew *comic book cover, published by the United States Air Force, 1964.*

tion markets, *Lost in Space* captures, like a flash of lightning in a bottle, the mood of a nation determined to land men on the moon before the decade of the sixties was out.

When *Lost in Space* debuted, a moon landing was four years away, but the contours of earlier space-traveling dreams had been fleshed out with the reality of manned orbital flights and satellite launches, unmanned probes sending back photographic images of the lunar surface, and visions of astronauts tethered to their orbiting ships and floating above Mother Earth.

DAWN OF THE SPACE AGE

The effort to construct a manned rocket for space travel began in 1926 when Robert Goddard launched the world's first liquid-propellant rocket from the snow-covered grounds of his Aunt Effie's farm. Although it only shot forty feet into the air, Goddard would write that it "looked almost magical as it rose."[1]

Another step into space was taken on October 14, 1947, when Air Force Captain Charles E. "Chuck" Yeager—progenitor of the line of space voyagers who had the "Right Stuff" (as writer Tom Wolfe famously dubbed the first flyguys to transition from fighter planes to rocket ships)—piloted his Bell X-1 662 miles an hour, breaking the sound barrier for the first time.

But the Space Age really arrived on October 4, 1957, the day the Soviet Union launched the first artificial satellite into Earth orbit, a twenty-three-inch-diameter sphere dubbed *Sputnik* ("traveling companion"). By September 14, 1959, the USSR's unmanned *Luna 2* spacecraft crashed on the distant lunar surface, making it the first space vehicle to reach the Moon. A month later, *Luna 3* would fly around the Moon and transmit the first images of its dark side.

The first living thing sent into orbit was an eleven-pound mongrel named Laika, with the ill-fated animal stuffed into *Sputnik II* and launched on November 3, 1957. (Laika would die within a week when the oxygen supply ran out, while the satellite itself stayed in orbit for 162 days before finally burning up in the atmosphere.)

The first human in space was Soviet cosmonaut Yuri Gagarin, who made the first manned orbital flight on April 12, 1961. The unfolding Space Race between the two post–World War II superpowers was joined when the United States launched astronaut Alan Shepard into space a month later. By 1965 the U.S. and Soviet space pro-

The work of visionary artists such as Chesley Bonestell literally illustrated the possibilities of space exploration. Bonestell's prophetic art featured orbiting space stations and space-walking astronauts in an influential series on space exploration that appeared in Collier's Magazine *during the early fifties. This Bonestell painting of a rocket ship and two astronauts on the moon helped George Pal sell his concept for* Destination Moon, *the 1950 feature that was inspired by the science of the day. (From the collection of Bob Burns, photo by Bruce Walters.)* (INSET) *Replica of final* Destination Moon *rocket ship with original miniature gantry from the 1950 film. (From the collection of Bob Burns, photo by Bruce Walters.)*

grams had both achieved orbital space walks.

In 1965 the U.S. had also shifted from its nascent Mercury program and into the Gemini missions (with a final Apollo phase designed to achieve the ultimate goal of a lunar touchdown). Also in 1965, "Early Bird," the world's first operational commercial communications satellite, was sent into orbit by the U.S.

TV'S FIRST FAMILY IN SPACE

Almost everything about space seemed possible in the midsixties. Movies and TV shows like *Lost in Space* were reflecting the wonder of it all. Even comic strip flatfoot Dick Tracy, who had long brandished that futuristic "two-way wrist radio," had turned his attention from the earthly underworld and begun patrolling the heavens in his Space

Coupe and fighting crime on the moon. In 1965 science fact and fiction writer Isaac Asimov seriously considered the possible physiognomy of a man from Mars (back then scientists considered Martian life unlikely, but not impossible).[2]

"Back then everyone was space-happy," notes Kevin Burns, a producer at Twentieth Century Fox's Foxstar Productions and a *Lost in Space* fan as a kid. "There was the possibility of the next frontier in movies like *Robinson Crusoe on Mars* [1964]. The 1960 Disney film *Swiss Family Robinson* [about a family marooned on an island] had also been popular, so it wasn't that big a leap for Irwin Allen to imagine Mr. and Mrs. America colonizing the new

Mark Goddard's hot-tempered mission copilot Major Don West.

The saboteur stowaway Dr. Zachary Smith, played by Jonathan Harris, was never identified as a Communist spy (presumably, by 1997 the Cold War would be settled—and they were right!), but his identification as an "agent of foreign powers" left no doubt to contemporary viewers as to Smith's origins. The *Jupiter 2*'s talking robot—who was simply called "Robot"—evolved in the storyline from Smith's mechanical puppet to Will's friend and guardian. (The Robot was animated by performer Bob May, who sat within the barrel-shaped robot suit, while the robotic voice-overs were supplied by Dick Tufeld.)

Executive producer Irwin Allen launched *Lost in Space* through Twentieth Century Fox Television

(ABOVE) *The* Jupiter 2 *men* (LEFT TO RIGHT)*: Major Don West (Mark Goddard), Will Robinson (Bill Mumy), and commander John Robinson (Guy Williams).* (RIGHT) *The* Jupiter 2 *women* (LEFT TO RIGHT)*: Penny Robinson (Angela Cartwright), Judy Robinson (Marta Kristen), and Maureen Robinson (June Lockhart).*

frontier of space like the pioneers that settled the West. I even have an old pitch tape for the series that actually said 'Mr. and Mrs. America will delight to the adventures . . . see *themselves* projected into space.'"

The show's cast featured Guy Williams (who had recently worn the black mask of TV's swashbuckling Zorro) as Professor John Robinson, with June Lockhart as John's adoring wife Maureen (America's TV mom had previously starred in *Lassie*). Their three children spanned the age range, with Marta Kristen as lovely Judy, Angela Cartwright as the prepubescent Penny, and Billy Mumy as plucky young Will. Assisting commander Robinson (and also charged with sparking a love interest with Judy) was actor

In the third season episode "Fugitives in Space," Dr. Zachary Smith (Jonathan Harris) finds himself on an interstellar chain gang with his nemesis, Major West. In the series saga, it was ironic that Smith's own fate would be linked with the crew whose mission he'd failed to destroy.

with a big-budget send-off. Although set in the then far-off future of 1997, the series didn't dwell on anticipating the possible science fact to come. From the black-and-white cliff-hanging thrills of the first season to the garish Pop Art color designs and campy humor of the final two seasons, the series used sci-fi themes as a springboard to realms of pure fantasy.

"*Lost in Space* aired at seven-thirty in the evening and was aimed at kids," recalls Len Brown, creative director at the Topps company, which produced a *Lost* TV tie-in trading card set. "I'm still a big fan of the Republic serials of the thirties and forties, and for me *Lost in Space* had the same flavor, with each hour episode having a cliffhanger ending. I was a big fan for its first season because I was a real science fiction fan and there wasn't that much TV science fiction on the three networks in 1965—even *Star Trek* was still a year away."

"In hindsight what was great about *Lost in Space* was the essence of the show was about the empowerment of the child," Kevin Burns adds. "As a kid watching the show I wasn't aware of the seams and papier-mâché props. It was just magical the way the show played to kids, hooking into their imagination. As a kid you could project yourself into the show. There was the little boy, Will, who could protect his family from chaos, Penny was there for the girls, and Judy was everybody's big sister. Kids watching that show in 1965 could imagine themselves in the future, in 1997, when they'd be about John Robinson's age. Kids could fantasize about traveling to the Moon with their own kids. Everything fell within the realm of possibility."

LOST IN TIME

That fateful Anno Domini has arrived and we're still far from the stars. The actual manned Moon explorations were conducted in a narrow window of time, from *Apollo 11*'s historic first lunar landing on July 20, 1969, to *Apollo 17*'s 1972 Christmas season voyage (with only *Apollo 13* forced to abort its lunar landing mission). Only twelve men, American astronauts all, have walked on the lunar surface.

Not only would Professor Robinson frown and shake his head at our failure of nerve in reaching for the stars, he'd be shocked by the likes of astronaut Shannon Lucid, a fifty-three-year-old who in 1996 spent a U.S.–record 188 days in space on *Mir* (Russian cosmonaut Valery Polyakov holds the record at 439 days). After all, it was the *men* who were in charge of the *Jupiter* settlement. While the womenfolk were of hardy pioneer stock, survival strategies were best charted by the alpha males.

Maureen Robinson also would be aghast at the real 1997, with its soaring divorce rates and single moms, dismayed that families rarely assemble around the communal table for the daily three squares. Maureen was one space mom who never let the rigors or terrors of an alien world keep her from tending the hydroponics garden or whipping up breakfast-lunch-and-dinner for everyone—irascible Dr. Smith included. (Many an episode was punctuated with Maureen's call: "Will, would you call in your sisters? Lunch is ready.")

Of course, 1965 was a different time for the *Lost in Space* creators and the entire country. Jim Crow segregation still held sway, forcing passage of the 1965 Voting Rights Act that allowed the registration of "Negro" voters, while the Watts race riot, which came days later, served notice that the long racial divide was not acceptable. In 1965 the first American combat troops, a force of 5,000 Marines, was sent to the jungles of Vietnam, a commitment that would escalate to 500,000 soldiers by early 1968.

In many ways the world has *completely* changed in the years since 1965. If one took time-lapse pictures, they'd show city skylines growing ever upward and once rural countrysides filling up with housing developments and strip malls. A time traveler might also note how America has become distrustful and cynical of the political institutions it once revered, how cloning and biotechnology are truly putting the tools of creation into human hands, and observe with awe the global influence of millennial megacorporations.

The popular culture's dreamscape has likewise been transformed. In the midsixties, the mediums of comic books and newspaper strips, trading cards, and science fiction and fantasy TV and movies were generally kid stuff. Today global entertainment and information companies have virtually replaced in importance the Machine Age industries of coal and steel. It's also no longer the "Big Three" networks that rule the broadcast waves, but super satellite systems transmitting hundreds of specialty cable channels. A single pop culture "property" can become a multimedia, multibillion-dollar enterprise spanning everything from movies and toys to fast food franchise tie-ins and licensed clothing lines.

Ironically, the Robinsons' mythical space launch year of 1997 also marked the production of a *Lost in Space* movie. The TV show had gotten by on shoestring budgets, with many an episode dressed up with recycled props and set pieces scavenged from the Fox back lot, with traditional effects work ranging from model ships flown on wires to actors dressing up in creature suits. In contrast, New Line Cinema's 1998 *LS* release was budgeted at an estimated $70 million dollars (an economical sum for an effects-heavy show), boast-

Maureen Robinson, space woman. Maureen spoke for the entire mission when, in the second episode ("The Derelict"), she said: "We're settlers, not explorers."

ed an all-star cast that included Oscar-winning actor William Hurt as John Robinson and Gary Oldman as Dr. Smith, and required eight soundstages at Shepperton Studios in England, more than 650 computer-generated animation shots, and the animatronic creature and robotics effects of Jim Henson's Creature Shop.

This book will be a timetraveling journey from the sixties to the nineties, with the *Jupiter 2* crew guiding us along the way. We'll contrast the dream of space travel and technology with the fantastic realities circa 1997 (as well as hear from an actual Moon walker, an astronaut whose lunar mission inspired a lifelong search to unlock the secrets of the universe). We'll also compare the pop cultural gestalt of the sixties with the high-powered multibillion-dollar entertainment industry of today.

We'll begin by going past that black-and-white world of the first *Lost in Space* season (when television was on the brink of flowering into a full-color medium) to the fifties, a time when a fantastic technofuture seemed to be taking form before one's eyes.

Back then there was still time to dream, to mentally prepare for the utopian, atomic-powered world of robot servants, moving sidewalks, personal helicopters for work commutes, orbiting space platforms, and especially those pleasure trips to the Moon.

① MYSTERY OF SPACE

LIFE IS WITH IT IN A FAR-OUT ERA

We begin this week to report the personal side of a story which we know will live on in history as long as there are men to record it. It is the story of the Astronauts—the supremely dramatic story of man's first efforts to leave his native Earth. . . . These remarkable human documents show the Astronauts are not only superb physical and psychological specimens but also thoughtful men. As one of them said, stepping from a training centrifuge after an eye-popping rise: "If any of us had begun to believe the stuff about our being supermen, we are learning different now."

—LIFE *MAGAZINE SERIES OF FIRST-PERSON REPORTS BY THE ASTRONAUTS,*
INTRODUCTORY EDITORIAL, SEPTEMBER 14, 1959

Space don't take too kindly to family outings. You're not out of gas on a highway back home, mister. You're way out yonder. And there ain't no highways way out yonder.

—WANDERING COWBOY ASTRONAUT JIMMY HAPGOOD TO MAJOR DON WEST IN
"WELCOME STRANGER," LOST IN SPACE EPISODE SIX, SEASON ONE

I n 1949 a Burbank teenager named Bob Burns walked on the Moon. He recalls the experience as a life-changing event.

This was a make-believe Moon, the lunar surface and starry sky erected on a soundstage set for producer George Pal's film *Destination Moon*. A dazzled Burns marked the visit as the beginning of a lifelong friendship with Pal (who would go on to create such famed science fiction films as *The War of the Worlds* and *The Time Machine*). Burns would ultimately pursue a colorfully eclectic Hollywood career, including perform-

ing effects work for American International Pictures (AIP) sci-fi/horror films and donning a gorilla suit to perform in such TV fare as the *Laugh-In* series.

DESTINATION MOON

"When I walked onto that Moon set it just blew my mind," Burns fondly recalls. "I knew then I had to be involved in the business somehow. I couldn't believe what I was seeing. The Moon set filled an entire soundstage, with a fabricated lunar surface and painted backdrops of the lunar mountains and stars beyond. I watched them film four actors dressed in

space suits and helmets exploring the moon. If you just concentrated on the set and didn't look at the lights and cameras, it really looked like you were on the Moon. *Destination Moon* was definitely a scientific re-creation—there were no Moon monsters or Moon babes."

Pal's film also showed astronauts floating weightless inside their ship (the performers flying by thin wires attached to special harnesses hidden underneath the space suit costumes) and a space walk sequence that predated the real thing by fifteen years (with cosmonaut Alexei A. Leonov doing the honors for real on March 18, 1965, and astro-

naut Ed White taking the first American space walk in June).

Destination Moon envisioned manned space-craft as a classic winged rocket ship capable of vertical takeoffs and planetary descents, unlike the *Apollo* multistage rockets that would ultimately allow for a capsule to be flown in Moon orbit while a pair of astronauts piloted a separate lunar module to the surface.

In Pal's film an early American test rocket blows up on the pad, which the heroes deduce to be sabotage (although this point is never proven or followed up on in the film). The incident captured

(ABOVE) *The set of George Pal's* Destination Moon, *the actual scene that a young, starstruck Bob Burns witnessed in 1949. As astronauts wait patiently in the background, the* Destination Moon *production crew commandeers the lunar surface in this 1949 "behind-the-scenes" image.* (BELOW) Destination Moon *film still, 1950. (Photos from the collection of Bob Burns.)*

the political paranoia of the emerging Cold War, which had begun heating up in 1949 when the Soviets exploded their first atomic bomb, ending America's exclusive membership in the Nuclear Club. The Soviet blockade of Berlin had also put the West on notice that communism was on the march, with the Kremlin at the controls.

The *Destination* moon shot is also spearheaded by private enterprise, not big government. During a pitch meeting to a room full of investors (and after an inexplicable Woody Woodpecker cartoon short has brought the money boys up to speed on the technology of space travel), a general gravely explains: "The race is on—and we'd better win it.

Because there's absolutely no way to stop an attack from outer space. The first country that can use the Moon for the launching of missiles will control the Earth! That, gentlemen, is the most important military fact of this century." The space dreamers get the money for their rocket ship.

The *Destination* rocket ship is built to use an "atomic energy engine," which generates fear about the health dangers of the "radioactive rocket" (the same concerns the public expressed for real in 1997 concerning the plutonium-powered Cassini space probe). Upon landing on the Moon and stepping onto its surface, one of the space travelers claims possession of the desolate world for the benefit of humankind and "by the grace of God and the name of the United States." After the mission, with Earth in sight of the returning rocket ship, the screen fills with the words: THIS IS THE END—OF THE BEGINNING.

FLIGHTS OF FANTASY

In recent centuries human beings began to get notions about voyaging off-world. In the sixteenth century French playwright Cyrano de Bergerac (immortalized centuries later in a drama by Edmond Rostand) prepared an unfinished novel, *Voyage to the Sun*, which imagined a solar-powered space vessel with windows that caught sun rays and

(OPPOSITE, CLOCKWISE FROM TOP) *A "planet X" that might be encountered by Earth's first interstellar travelers, as envisioned by artist Harry Lange for the Winter 1959 issue of* Space Journal. *This cover painting and article wasn't a flight of science fancy but a serious hypothesis of the possible look of an alien world "in a stage of evolution younger than Earth. . . ." For* Space Journal *article, Lange imagines space travelers assembling a "photon thrust unit" in planetary orbit to propel the spacecraft to the speed of light, or close enough to overcome "time and man's limited life span." Planet X landing and take-off vehicle.*

● THE NECESSITY OF SPACE TRAVEL — BY DR. PHILIP N. SHOCKEY
● DYNAMICS OF LIFE IN THE UNIVERSE — BY JOHN HULLEY
● RELATIVITY AND SPACE FUNDAMENTALS — BY JAMES P. GARDNER
● THE RADIATION HAZARD TO SPACE TRAVEL — BY DR. JAN S. PAUL
● DESIGN FOR BUILDINGS ON THE MOON — BY DR. JOHN S. RINEHART
● SURVIVAL IN SPACE — BY DR. SIEGFRIED J. GERATHEWOHL

SPACE JOURNAL

DEDICATED TO THE ASTRO-SCIENCES

MARCH-MAY   WINTER ● 50c

For an Uncreased Cover, Send 25c to Space Enterprises,
Box 94, Nashville, Tenn.

PROJECT STAR ● LANDING ON PLANET ONE HUNDRED MILLION YEARS YOUNGER THAN EARTH

SPACE JOURNAL PROUDLY PRESENTS ARTIST HARRY LANGE'S PANORAMA OF EARTH'S FIRST INTERSTELLAR SPACE SHIP (DESIGNED BY ASTRONAUTICAL ENGINEERS HELMUT HOEPFNER AND B. SPENCER ISBELL) LANDING IN ANOTHER SOLAR SYSTEM. WITH A DEFT HAND AND PAINSTAKING CARE FOR AUTHENTIC DETAIL, LANGE HAS CAPTURED THE FASCINATING SCENE ENVISIONED BY DR. PHILIP SHOCKEY IN "THE NECESSITY OF SPACE TRAVEL" APPEARING IN THIS EDITION. SHOCKEY SUGGESTS THE PROBABILITY THAT SHOULD EARTHMANS' FIRST INTERSTELLAR SPACE TRAVELERS FIND A PLANET WITH NEAR-EARTH ENVIRONMENTAL CONDITIONS, THE PLANET WOULD NOT BE IN THE SAME EVOLUTIONARY STAGE AS EARTH. THIS RENDERING SHOWS THE DESTINATION PLANET IN ITS CRETACEOUS PERIOD OF DEVELOPMENT, THE MONSTERS CREATED BY NATURE AND MAN STAND IN STARK CONTRAST.

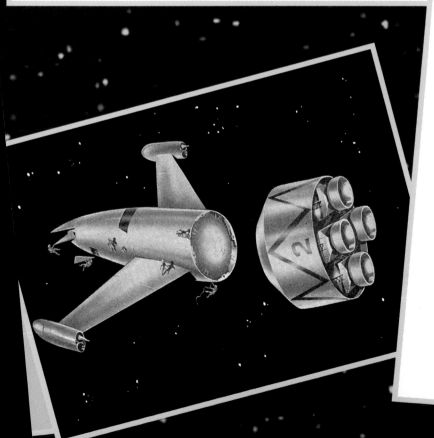

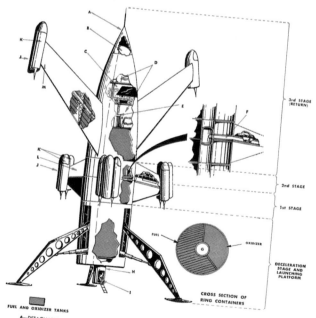

PLANET "X" LANDING AND TAKE-OFF VEHICLE
ASTRA-α-001

3rd STAGE (RETURN)

2nd STAGE

1st STAGE

FUEL   OXIDIZER

DECELERATION STAGE AND LAUNCHING PLATFORM

CROSS SECTION OF RING CONTAINERS

FUEL AND OXIDIZER TANKS

A—DETACHABLE NOSE CONE
B—RE-ENTRY NOSE CONE
C—CONTROL ROOM
D—CREW QUARTERS
E—ELEVATOR ENTRANCE
F—ENGINE ACCESS TUNNEL

G—ELEVATOR SHAFT
H—TELESCOPING ELEVATOR SECTION
I—ELEVATOR EXIT
J—CONVENTIONAL ROCKET ENGINES
K—COMBINATION TURBO-RAM JET ENGINES
L—FINS/OUTRIGGERS
M—WINGS/OUTRIGGERS

BUCK ROGERS DREAMS

The name "Buck Rogers" is synonymous with swashbuckling space travel and all the glittering wonders of the imagined technofuture: skyscraper cities designed with superfreeways navigated by floating cars, "television view plates," advanced radio technologies, rocket guns, and "jumping belts" (which, thanks to the synthetic element *inertron*, allows the wearer to defy gravity and fall *away* from the Earth's center).

Perhaps less known is that Rogers (introduced as a newspaper comic strip character in 1929) had a lot of the old Rip Van Winkle in him: After serving as a World War I fighter pilot, the twenty-year-old Buck was hired to survey an abandoned mine near Pittsburgh, where a cave-in and a strange gas cloud caused him to lose consciousness. When Buck awakened, he found himself in the fantastic twenty-fifth century. ("The peculiar gas which had defied chemical analysis, preserved me in suspended animation," Buck helpfully noted in the inaugural strip.)

The early *Buck Rogers* adventures would probably be deemed a little too extravagant for sensitive modern tastes, notably those Mongol hordes who sought to enslave all fair-skinned humanity. Other tales were far-

allowed the collected heat to expand a globe and lift off and up into space. It was a fairly advanced notion, since at the time it was believed that birds hibernated on the Moon and conveyances could reach space while carried on the wings of birds. By the seventeenth and eighteenth centuries variants of hot air balloons were considered as possible space-traveling vehicles, while in the nineteenth century it was even supposed that passengers could be loaded into cannons and simply shot into space. Serious thought was also given to storing provisions aboard a craft, the probable cold of space, and even the weightlessness that would be experienced beyond the pull of gravity.

Modern science fiction was arguably born with the coming of the French writer Jules Verne (1828–1905) and the English writer H. G. Wells (1866–1946). Among their many works, both men

imagined voyages to the Moon, with Jules Verne publishing his *From the Earth to the Moon* in 1865, while Wells's *The First Men in the Moon* was released in 1901.

Then the twentieth century ushered in the moving pictures, the perfect medium for presenting tales of fantasy and science fiction. French filmmaker Georges Méliès's famed 1902 release *A Trip to the Moon*, at some twenty-one minutes an extravaganza for the times (with most films then running one to three minutes), featured a shot of a cannon-propelled, bullet-shaped capsule landed smack in the right eye of the man in the moon. That image, both comical and surreal, is one of the most famous single images in movie history.

By the early fifties the Atomic Age had arrived, commercial air travel had advanced, and the evolution of rocket science made a lunar expe-

fetched in imagining possible futures: In one 1939 tale a team of Solar Scouts on Mars discovers the sunken wreck of an Earth-to-Mars expedition ambitiously launched in 1949.

But Buck, with his wild escapades and travels to exotic planets, struck a nerve precisely because his adventures were such fantastical stuff. Back in 1929 commercial radio was in its infancy, television still in the domain of mad science laboratories, tape recorders were unknown. In the U.S. there were no cross-country freeways or streamlined bullet trains. The idea of flying a craft that could crack the sound barrier seemed impossible, much less notions of manning a rocket and blasting off from Earth.

Even by the forties and fifties, "Buck Rogers" was still a clarion call to imagine the impossible. Bob Burns heard and remembers, with his boyhood collection of Buck Rogers ray guns and a beloved Buck Rogers helmet still in his possession. "I loved that helmet so much I'd wear it to bed at night," Burns laughs. "Then my mom would come in and make me take it off. But as soon as she left the room I'd put it back on. I'm sure part of the attraction was escapism, but another part of it was these space heroes were so cool. I'd always play Buck Rogers when I was a kid, especially when I put the helmet on. I not only wanted to be like Buck Rogers, I wanted to be *better* than Buck— I wanted to be 'Two Dollar Rogers!'"

In a corner of one of his home display cases is Bob Burns's beloved childhood Buck Rogers helmet, dressed out on a mannequin head (along with other classic pop dolls, trinkets, and toys).

dition not only possible but seemingly inevitable. Thus, fictional works such as *Destination Moon* began to look less like fantasy and more like prophecy.

Of course, in most dimensions of pop culture those "moon babes" still reigned supreme. You didn't have to be a rocket scientist to enjoy these tall tales of the early Space Age—you just had to be a space cadet. Intermingling with those fantastic space heroes were serious musings about the qualities of the prototypical space man who would blaze the off-world trail.

SPACE CADETS

In 1949, when commercial television was new and primitive, one of the medium's wonders was *Captain Video*, the first science fiction show on TV. The exploits of the "Master of the Stratosphere" were broadcast weekly in five thirty-minute black-and-white episodes. Bob Burns, who faithfully

Space cadets relax in this scene from the Tom Corbett *TV series.*

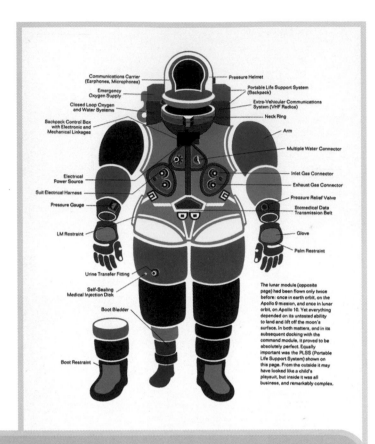

Labels on image 1:
Communications Carrier (Earphones, Microphones)
Emergency Oxygen Supply
Closed Loop Oxygen and Water Systems
Backpack Control Box with Electronic and Mechanical Linkages
Electrical Power Source
Suit Electrical Harness
Pressure Gauge
LM Restraint
Urine Transfer Fitting
Self-Sealing Medical Injection Disk
Boot Bladder
Boot Restraint

Pressure Helmet
Portable Life Support System (Backpack)
Extra-Vehicular Communications System (VHF Radios)
Neck Ring
Arm
Multiple Water Connector
Inlet Gas Connector
Exhaust Gas Connector
Pressure Relief Valve
Biomedical Data Transmission Belt
Glove
Palm Restraint

The lunar module (opposite page) had been flown only twice before: once in earth orbit, on the Apollo 9 mission, and once in lunar orbit, on Apollo 10. Yet everything depended on its untested ability to land and lift off the moon's surface. In both matters, and in its subsequent docking with the command module, it proved to be absolutely perfect. Equally important was the PLSS (Portable Life Support System) shown on this page. From the outside it may have looked like a child's playsuit, but inside it was all business, and remarkably complex.

(TOP) *Apollo-era space suit.* (Look Special: Apollo 11 On The Moon.) (BELOW) *The idealized "space-crew candidate" imagined at the dawn of the Space Age by artist Virgil Finlay for* The Complete Book of Space Travel.

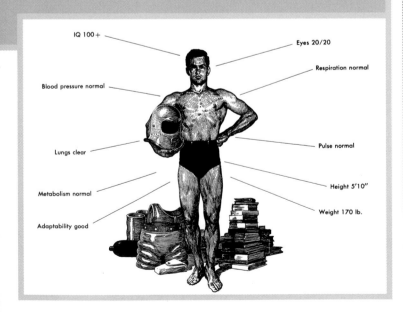

Labels on image 2:
IQ 100+
Blood pressure normal
Lungs clear
Metabolism normal
Adaptability good
Eyes 20/20
Respiration normal
Pulse normal
Height 5'10"
Weight 170 lb.

watched the show as a kid, recalls how cool it all was—and how forgiving a young fan could be in putting up with the sometimes unexpected travails the Captain and his Video Rangers encountered each week. "Captain Video was the guardian of the universe, but it was a really cheap show," Burns recalls, laughing, "with cardboard sets and alien creatures that would basically be some guy wearing a Halloween mask and a couple of horns. Plus, each show was broadcast live! There were a lot of goofs on the air and they couldn't do anything about it."

Burns recalls witnessing several classic on-air blunders on *Tom Corbett, Space Cadet,* another live sci-fi show of the early fifties. "I remember one show where Tom Corbett is in his space ship *Polaris* and he's talking to this gal who's a scientist or something, and he starts to go down the hatch of his ship. What they always did in those instances was the hatch opening only went down a few feet, so the camera would cut away and the actors would hurry over to another set. Well, as Tom starts to go down the hatch his foot gets caught and he moves the hatch about three feet! Of course they acted like it didn't happen but you couldn't help but notice. But as a kid I thought it was cool—that's a set!

"On another episode the head commander is talking to Tom Corbett and they're wearing their uniforms with these ornate gauntleted gloves on. Somehow their arms touched and they got caught in each other's gloves! They gamely went on with their dialogue while they struggled to get uncaught. Finally they ended up ripping themselves apart. It was very funny."

While the popular culture was having its way in space, scientists and science writers were busily thinking through the dynamic of bringing off a successful launch, lunar landing, and return. Would too much acceleration pulverize and splatter the flesh of the space crew? Would weightless conditions wreak havoc on too-weak flesh? Others pondered the possibility of life on Mars and the other worlds that might prove an eventual destination for the space explorers.

The Complete Book of Space Travel, published in 1956, suggested that the space traveler applicant pool would initially number in the tens of thousands before being winnowed down to several dozen perfect specimens of terrestrial manhood. "We want, above all, to know if there are intelligent beings like ourselves elsewhere in the universe," author Albro T. Gaul suggested. "If we do meet intelligent creatures, our first space crew will be earth's ambassadors. Truly they must be earth's finest."[1]

In the gung-ho spirit of the day, either an orbiting space platform or a lunar colony would be established to facilitate voyages to other worlds. The chance of encountering alien life during the colonization of space was also a real possibility. Even the danger of space travel was nothing compared to the alien microorganisms of another world.

"We shall train our spacemen to have better sense than to eat anything they see alive on alien soils," noted *The Complete Book of Space Travel*. "But there is one danger which we cannot learn about in training. This is disease. Even if there were a race of intelligent Martians, either still alive, or long since extinct, it would make very little difference to us if we died of Martian diseases before we could protect ourselves. It is quite within the realm of possibility that there exist on other planets simple forms of life that could find a ready host in human subjects. . . . This is definitely a problem to consider, but we shall never know the answer until we get there."[2]

Regardless, America's reveries of space travel were shattered in 1957 when the Soviet Union put the first artificial satellite into planetary orbit and truly ushered in the Space Age.

SOUNDS OF SPUTNIK

In the August 5, 1955, issue of *U.S. News & World Report*, a special section on the coming age of orbiting satellites projected that between July 1957 and December 1958 the U.S. would launch a satellite. Rocket science had progressed to the point where it was only a question of when—and whether the Soviets would beat America into orbit.

"Questions already are being raised as to whether some of the persistent 'flying saucer' reports may not have been caused by sightings of unannounced satellites, possibly launched by the Russians," the magazine mused. "Many of the Russians' top scientists are known to be working now on the [satellite] project. . . . Just how far they

"Sputnik: One Reason Why We Lost," cover article for 1958 issue of Fantasy and Science Fiction. *The Soviet Union's successful launching of* Sputnik I, *the world's first artificial satellite, officially kicked off the Space Age—and heated up Cold War fever in the United States (*Explorer 1, *America's first successful satellite, would be launched from Cape Canaveral, Florida, on January 31, 1958.)*

THE ART OF EXPLOITATION

The fifties and sixties was the era of the "exploitation film" in all its gaudy glory. These down-and-dirty productions mainlined into juicy, provocative themes, the stuff of yellow journalism and bloody pulp magazines, and were sold to wide-eyed youngsters using provocative, pulse-pounding titles and poster art. We're talking here about the likes of American International Pictures, home to Roger Corman and the classic formula of low budgets, fast shoots, and lucrative profit margins.

The 1957 comedy/sci-fi production *Invasion of the Saucer-Men*, which featured big-brained aliens with needlelike fingers able to inject alcohol into teenage victims, did boast some top-of-the-line production values, particularly in the creation of a wooded area in which the action played out. "That *Saucer-Men* set was one of the best sets I've ever been on," notes Bob Burns, who worked on the film during an AIP career that began on the sidelines of the 1956 Corman film *The Day the World Ended*. "These films had art directors who would design the stuff and set personnel to create it. These guys were very, very good at their craft. They called up greenery places to rent all the real trees and foliage they needed to dress out the set. When you were on that set you really felt like you were out in the woods."

Burns recalls that he and veteran AIP effects artist Paul Blaisdell did all the effects for *Invasion of the Saucer-Men*—in one day! Working on an insert stage, the area reserved for close-ups and effects work, the duo created such shots as an alien poking a victim's neck with an alcohol-tipped finger (with Burns himself taking it in the neck with a retractable needle gag) and a gory effect of a Saucer-Man's eye poked out by a bull's horn (with Burns using a bull's horned head on a rod and Blaisdell operating a hero Saucer head on a rig, while a grease gun full of chocolate syrup, injected from behind the alien head's wounded eye, supplied the spurt of blood). The flying saucer itself, which would be flown on wires, was carved out of white pine and layered to a metallic-looking finish with 100 coats of paint.

Burns claims that *Saucer-Men*, with its subplot of the government's cover-up of the saucer crash, was one of the first films to exploit the specter of governmental conspiracies. "In the fifties there was fear of atomic war, the Big Red scare and the Cold War," says Burns. "Paranoia was running rampant. So a lot of the exploitation films, like *Saucer-Men*, were made with that in mind. And of course there was always the idea that men would band together to destroy the Big Menace—like the teenagers who destroy the Saucer-Men in the end."

Unlike their tonier counterparts, an AIP production didn't need to spend years to develop a property and write a script. Why wait when the concept would write itself? "James Nicholson, the head of AIP, would come up with titles like *The She Creature*, *It Conquered the World*, *Invasion of the Saucer-Men*, and *I Was a Teenage Werewolf*, and they'd do a story around them," recalls Burns. "You're a kid and you see a movie poster with a title like *The She Creature*, and you have to see it! Of course, you were always disappointed, but you still saw them."

A classic truth-in-advertising poster produced by American Releasing Corporation (which would be renamed AIP) was produced for that 1955 tale of an "Unspeakable Horror," the widescreen saga filmed in "Terror-scope"—*The Beast with 1,000,000 Eyes!* The monster on the poster, while not pictured with a million eyes, showed promise with nine bloodshot orbs. But the monster actually seen in the movie, created as a hand puppet effect by Paul Blaisdell, seemingly shortchanged audiences by 998,000 eyes.

"They always had to explain that the beast in the movie was the *slave* of the beast with a million eyes," Burns laughs. "The beast was actually this invisible entity who could control millions of minds—that's where the 'million eyes' came in. That was always the bone of contention. Nobody knew this creature was the slave. It even had chains on it! But nobody saw that."

Regardless, the exploitation formula worked for a long time. "AIP made a lot of money and was one of the busiest studios in the fifties doing these science fiction/horror films," Burns sums up. "Almost every one of these films was shot in about seven days. It was like an ensemble thing because you almost always had the same crew from film to film. We had a fellow named Eddie Cahn, an old western director, who could do like seventy to eighty setups in a day [as opposed to the average of fifteen to twenty a day]! The spirit was, 'Let's go out and do a show!'"

(OPPOSITE) Invasion of the Saucer-Men *one-sheet poster for 1957 film.* (TOP) *In this 1957 shot, Bob Burns* (LEFT) *holds a "crawling hand" and Paul Blaisdell a disembodied Saucer head. In the foreground is a miniature of the alien spacecraft that brought the "creeping horror" to Earth.* (ABOVE) *The Venusian monster, another Blaisdell creation, gets a grip on Lee Van Cleef in American International's* It Conquered the World *(1956). Van Cleef would go on to filmdom immortality as the "Bad" equation in the Sergio Leone spaghetti western classic* The Good, the Bad, and the Ugly.

have gotten, however, is still a mystery."

But the heart of the matter was revealed in this comment in that 1955 *U.S. News* issue: "When a satellite actually is launched, how far behind will be the military space platforms, and who will man them?"

So it was that America and the world were shocked when, on October 4, 1957, the Soviets shot *Sputnik* in orbit. *Sputnik* was a sphere, twenty-three inches in diameter and weighing less than two hundred pounds, with four nine-foot antennas. The satellite orbited at a range of 156 to 560 miles above Earth and at speeds of 18,000 miles per hour. The sphere made a complete orbit every ninety-six minutes, all the while beeping radio signals down to Earth. After ninety-two days in orbit, the satellite finally gave in to the pull of gravity and burned up in the atmosphere.

In that autumn of 1957 there was anguish in America that Uncle Sam had lost the "satellite race." The stakes had been high: The rocket force required for blasting a satellite into orbit meant that the Russians had cleared a major hurdle in the development of an intercontinental ballistic missile. Once the remaining technical problems of guidance and atmospheric reentry were solved, it would be possible to launch a missile from Moscow to New York.

(ABOVE) *Cosmonaut Yuri Gagarin surveys Earth from the orbiting* Vostok I *capsule. (Two-page spread from a special booklet on Gagarin, ©Novosti Press Agency Publishing House 1977).* (BELOW) *"Rocket War," cover article,* Look, *July 31, 1951. The anticipated journey "to the stars" could not shake the dark cloud of the Cold War era. This Chesley Bonestell splash page drawing of a satellite augurs, in writer Willy Ley's words, "vast possibilities for war."*

When *Sputnik* was announced, a teenage ham radio enthusiast in Los Angeles named Merrill Dean was at the controls of his Hammarlund radio set. Dean was listening for the sounds of *Sputnik* passing overhead, waiting with a reel-to-reel tape recorder to capture the pulses of the first man-made signals from space.

Dean, whose eventual career would range from Walt Disney Company executive to running a global Internet business in 1997, still is a ham radio enthusiast and credits his international business acumen to his youthful ham experiences talking with other operators around the planet. Dean, who had a youthful fascination with ray-beam devices and other science fiction stuff, was fascinated with the magic of wireless communication.

"I was intrigued with the notion of getting a signal from nowhere," Dean says, smiling. "A few years before I got into ham radio I built a crystal set, a little piece of germanium diode onto which you put a little wire to pick up a normal AM radio signal that you can then listen to through earphones. This was all still the vacuum tube technology from the thirties, which didn't change until the solid-state electronics and silicon transistors, which came in around 1956."

In that presatellite world, long before the

communications satellites and instantaneous global communication to come, the ham radio set was a way of spanning the planet. "A ham radio is a very mystical thing," Dean explains. "It was amazing to me that you could project your voice all over the world just using signals bouncing off of the ionosphere. The sun ionizes the ionosphere and makes these signals bounce, instead of just going out into outer space, which happens to the magnetic waves coming off regular radio and TV transmission. Ham radio communications are instantaneous—the speed of light. So I can be talking to a ham operator in Japan and the signal is over in a heartbeat. The only limit is you have to wait for the sun to ionize the ionosphere in a particular part of the world, so certain frequencies are open to you during the night, others during the day."

It was while talking to some English-speaking ham operators in Russia that Dean heard that *Sputnik* was in orbit. Dean was given the frequency from which the satellite was sending signals. Then he settled in, anxiously waiting for the Soviet sphere to fly over his Los Angeles home.

"At first I heard nothing but white noise," Dean recalls. "Then all of a sudden I could hear this faint *beep-beep-beep*. And as it got closer it got louder and when it was directly overhead it was the loudest. Then the signal got weaker and weaker as it passed on, then disappeared. I taped the signal on reel-to-reel and sent it to Cal Tech. I'm not sure what they did with it, but the whole experience was a big thrill."

According to international ham radio etiquette, confirmation of radio contact is made with the exchange of a QSL international code card. Ham radio operators around the world who had tuned in and listened to *Sputnik*'s transmissions received a special confirm card from their radio buddies in the Soviet Union. "Everybody who sent a QSL card to a ham radio guy in Russia got a card back with a little picture of the *Sputnik*," Dean smiles. "This tiny metallic sphere with antenna. I've still got my *Sputnik* card."

Teenage ham radio jockey Merrill Dean was tuned in as Sputnik *passed over his Los Angeles home, and later received this QSL card and notice from his ham radio friends in Moscow.*

JONATHAN HARRIS

When Stephen Hopkins, director of the *Lost in Space* movie, telephoned Jonathan Harris about a possible cameo in the New Line feature, the inestimable Mr. Harris demurred, "I play Smith or I don't play." Although the role of Dr. Smith was already spoken for (with Gary Oldman in the part), Harris retains a special identification with the character he created.

The origin of saboteur Smith is the stuff of showbiz legend: the character was added to a revamped *Lost in Space* pilot (along with the Robot) by CBS brass who felt the series needed something more than the weekly adventure Irwin Allen had planned for a marooned space family, the Robinsons. But Harris, ever the savvy veteran performer, saw professional doom in the sinister Smith. "He was so dark and terrible," Harris recalls, "that I thought the Robinsons would have to kill him off within five episodes. Unemployed again?! So I decided to sneak in the things for which I'm justly famous—comedic villainy. A villain who's also funny becomes quite redeemable in the eyes of the audience."

Today Harris's career (which includes, by his estimate, more than six hundred different television episodes) rolls on. Although nowadays he turns down live performances, he's become a popular voice actor for many animated productions (including Pixar's upcoming film, *A Bug's Life*).

Perhaps less known is Harris's work as a stage performer, particularly a Broadway career that lasted from the early 1940s through the mid-1950s. Harris performed in such plays as Truman Capote's *The Grass Harp* (during which he recalls the eccentric writer appearing at the opening "wearing a mustard-colored velvet suit with a royal chiffon scarf") and worked with the likes of Lillian Gish, Helen Hayes, and a young Marlon Brando. "Marlon was *wonderful* to behold—that passion is a gift. You don't come by that naturally, it just descends upon you," says Harris.

Harris's life as an actor is full of anecdotes that trace his early days on the Broadway stage and a fateful detour through Hollywood.

I made my Broadway debut in 1942 in a play called **The Heart of a City** *at the Henry Miller Theater on 43rd Street. Talk about nervous excitement! I was hysterical. My Broadway debut! God save us. I played a Polish flyer in the RAF! I got the part because I hounded the office of the producer, Gilbert Miller. I had no agent, as I was a beginner, and the office secretary would throw me out: "Go! Nothing for you." But young, ambitious, and tough as nails, I'd come back the next day. Finally, after weeks, I think she got bored seeing me and finally told me to sit down and wait. I waited for hours and finally she said, "Five minutes." I walked in and there was Mr. Miller, the great man behind a big desk. I told him I knew there was a part for me in his play. "Hmmmm," he said. "There's a little part, couple of lines. Pays scale. Tell her!" I nearly died. I told her, and I thought she was going to slap my face for daring to get a job without her sanction. She gave me a script and said, "By the way, you're going to play the flyer with a Polish accent. You got one?" "Well, yes," I said. I walked out and said to myself, "Polish accent? What the fuck is that?"*

But my mind was working. I knew there had to be a Polish consulate in New York City and that's where I'd get my Polish accent. I arrived at the consulate and a charming lady behind a desk, who sounded French to me, introduced me around. While everyone sounded un-American, every accent was totally different. Nobody sounded quite "Polish." The woman told me the accent depended on where you lived, your education, and your travels. I went home and put together all these strange sounds I'd heard. And then the fateful day of my first Broadway rehearsal approached. Let me tell you, **terror struck!**

A group of nervous actors showed up on the stage of the 43rd Street theater with Miller and his associates sitting in the dark in the house proper. The seating was wood-backed chairs arranged in a sort of semicircle; the

Actor Jonathan Harris transformed sinister saboteur Zachary Smith, here pondering his next move with his Robot agent of destruction, into an inimitable personification of comedic villainy.

lighting, a 500-watt bulb hanging suspended in a wire cage, threw ghastly shadows on the actor's faces. Inside I was shaking like a leaf. Finally my cue comes and I gird my loins—this is engraved in blood in my head—and I say my lines with my "authentic Polish accent." I don't fall off my chair, I don't fumble my lines, thank you God. We finish the play, Gilbert Miller thanks everyone, and then he points at **me**: "You! Come here!" "Oh God," I'm thinking, "he's got me. **He knows!**" I went over and Miller asks me where I got the accent. Well, I told my first marvelous lie: "Mr. Miller, I come by it naturally. You see, my parents are Polish and that's the way they sound." He waited for a moment then turned to his associate and said, "Five dollars! I told you I could spot a real one!" Ha! I love it. Never forgot it. I've used that Polish accent to play everything from an Arab and a Hindustani to a Jewish rabbi and an Irish patriot. Works like a charm!

You know, I have an affinity for acting, but that doesn't alter the terror. Do you realize what happens to us actors on opening night? It's almost a disease. I did a play with Helen Hayes and we were waiting to make our

entrance when I looked at her and she looked like I looked: absolutely waxen. I leaned over and whispered to her, "Still, Miss Hayes?" And she looked up at me and replied, "Gets worse every year." This was the Helen Hayes, a great star. But as your reputation grows, other people can blow a line—but not the star!

I once was in a play called **A Flag Is Born** with Paul Muni and Marlon Brando. It was written by Ben Hecht and had a symphony orchestra, with Luther Adler directing. I was the understudy to Muni and his character was a monstrously long part: a very old man with a heavy makeup, a beard, and a leonine wig. Happily, Muni would let me come in and worship in his dressing room. I'd come to the theater, put my face on, then fly to his dressing room, and I wouldn't say a word. As he'd talk I'd watch him like a hawk. I certainly learned makeup from him— you know, in the theater we do it ourselves. Then came the day I took over for Muni. The night before—the terror! This was Broadway, my dream, in full view of everybody. I was up all night going over my lines.

The night of my performance I was in the wings waiting for my cue. Behind me was Celia Adler—a lovely little lady, like a bird—who played my wife. And my cue came—and my cue went. And there I stood. And stood. And stood. Unable to move! So scared, I can feel it now. Bless her heart, Celia, I'll never be able to thank her enough—I think she's gone now—she picked up her foot, placed it right in my ass, and **propelled** me onto the stage. I stumbled on, which was fine since it was very much a part of the character. And then I was off, didn't blow a single line.

My first movie was **Botany Bay**, directed by John Farrow, who's Mia's dad. The film starred Alan Ladd, James Mason, and me. I was the "New York actor," so referred to by Mr. Farrow, who was not an adorable man. Far from it! I don't believe he liked actors, you see, which is a very serious failing for a director. It was a hell of an introduction to Hollywood. I was fresh off the Broadway stage where we all loved each other and here was this dreadful, dreadful man! Almost nobody escaped from that vitriolic and sly tongue.

One day he verbally attacked James Mason on the set of the bridge of a full-size ship, which by the way was complete in every detail, sailing in ten feet of water on a Paramount soundstage with a giant process screen behind it—I was overwhelmed, I tell you! HOLLYWOOD! So Farrow went to work on Mason as I watched from afar. Nothing happened and about twenty minutes later James said to Farrow, "Did you say something to me, sir?" Farrow knew when he was licked. So, that was kind of joyous.

Well, about two weeks before the film wrapped, the William Morris agency, which represented me at the time, called me about being on a nine-month shoot with Spencer Tracy. My idol! I thought he was the best movie actor in the world. The film was being directed by Clarence Brown, who was a powerful, well-known director, but I knew nothing else about him. Now, after being with Farrow, I was a little gun-shy. So I called my friend Rock Hudson—darling, sweet, gentle soul, and I miss him—and I said, "Rock, two words: **Clarence Brown!**" And Rock says, "You are working at Paramount with John Farrow? Well, John Farrow is Shirley Temple next to Clarence Brown!" That was all I needed. I went right back to New York to work on Truman Capote's play **The Grass Harp**. But that was a serious career mistake. Nine months with Spencer Tracy! I would have learned so much. But I felt I had to go back where I belonged. This was 1954.

Well, it's been a vast career. I've been very lucky, but everything I've ever done has come to an end. The curtain always comes down, the shoot finishes. "Next!" What is next? Then the telephone rings and your life changes. But the life of the stage is finished for me now. It was a great life and I adored it. But I'm still a wonderful audience. I go to the theater all the time.

I love a curtain going up and down. Perhaps it's childish, I admit it, but I want to be on the stage when the curtain rises. It's a feeling that puts me away. Up goes the curtain, the bank of lights in the balcony comes on, and we're off. It's Heaven. Oh, I loved it! Magic time!

According to Topps executive Len Brown, who wrote the backs of the Outer Limits cards, the stories had no resemblance to the actual TV episodes. ("Man from Tomorrow," Outer Limits #50, 1964, Bubbles, Inc. [Topps].)

MAN FROM TOMORROW

⊋ *THIRD EYE CULTURE*

> *The Man from the Future continues speaking to the people of today's Earth . . . There is a threat, he warns, of atomic war which will cost every country untold losses . . . And with that The Man from Tomorrow vanishes. Immediately the leaders of Earth meet and begin building for greater understanding and toward peace that all men desire.*
>
> —"MAN FROM TOMORROW," THE OUTER LIMITS *TV TRADING CARD COPY, #50, 1964, BUBBLES, INC. (AKA TOPPS)*

Lost in Space was broadcast at a technological turning point for TV. Only a few years before the show's debut, the medium was still being likened to visual radio, with most programs still broadcast in black and white by the mid-sixties. By its second season, *Lost in Space* transitioned to color, thanks in part to the increasing affordability of home color sets. The monochromatic palette of American popular culture suddenly became drenched in color, from the bright primary color schemes of the Pop Art movement and the psychedelic rainbow hues of acid rock light shows and poster art to the visual "Pow!" of the live-action comic book *Batman* ABC TV show (which for a time competed with *Lost in Space* in its Wednesday time slot).

The all-color tube was arguably the beginning of a shift in pop cultural consciousness. The kid stuff of old would eventually become the "properties" of the adult world.

REMEMBERING THE GOLDEN AGE

In his classic 1965 book *The Great Comic Book Heroes*, Jules Feiffer poignantly recalled the "Golden Age" of comics, that era in the late thirties through the forties when caped and cowled

MAD NEW WORLD
of Batman, Superman
and the Marquis de Sade

Batman makes
a mighty leap into
national popularity

MARCH 11 · 1966 · 35¢

In its second season time slot, Lost in Space *got some competition from* Batman. *With its camp irony, bright color schemes, and "Pow" emblazoned scenes, it was indeed, as this* Life *cover noted, a "mad new world"—and the pop cultural gestalt would never be the same.*

superheroes took on all comers, even Hitler's fascist hordes. Lamenting the comics censorship crackdowns of the fifties, which even included a highly publicized Congressional investigation, Feiffer sighed at the temerity of adults invading the inner sanctum of a kid's fantasy world. Adults said comics were junk. Of course. That was precisely the point.

"With [comics] we were able to roam free, disguised in costume, committing the greatest of feats—and the worst of sins," Feiffer wrote. "And, in every instance, getting away with them. For a little while, at least, it was our show. . . . Psychically renewed, we could then return above ground and put up with another couple of days of victimization. Comic books were our booze."[1]

The censorship travails required a "Comics Code Authority" emblem to be printed on every approved comics issue. Then things settled back to kid stuff as usual, albeit watered down. But by the midsixties the icons of pop culture were starting to appear, blown up bigger than life, in the mainstream culture.

It was a revelation for comics fans to not only experience the comic book heroics of *Batman* as a live-action TV show, but also see the new aes-

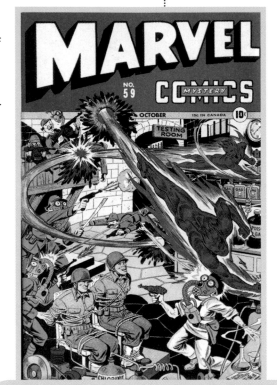

It was no coincidence that the "Golden Age" of the comic book superheroes coincided with the onslaught of World War II. On this fictional plane the superhero forces helped turn the tide against the Axis hordes, as the Human Torch and his sidekick Toro demonstrate in this 1944 Marvel Mystery Comics *cover by Alex Schomburg.* ©*Marvel Entertainment Group, Inc.*

thetic celebrated on the cover of *Life* magazine (with the image of Bat-costumed star Adam West leaping amid floating bat logos and the cover copy stating: "Batman makes a mighty leap into national popularity").[2]

Of course, there was still the occasional aberration that popped up to shock the elders of the culture, notably the big-headed alien invaders of *Mars Attacks!*

THE THIRD EYES

In 1962 astronaut John Glenn orbited Earth for nearly five hours. That same year the Topps Chewing Gum Company, noted for its baseball cards and TV tie-in cards, released a fifty-five-card set titled *Mars Attacks!* The cards featured Martians with big exposed brains and skeletal faces who wreaked absolute havoc on terrestrial life and property. The Martians exploded the Empire State Building and the Golden Gate Bridge, released giant insects to feast on human victims, and turned their death rays on anything that moved—even incinerating a little dog in one particularly infamous card.

The company had tried to deflect any possible controversy by labeling the cards with the pseudonym "Bubbles, Inc.," but to no avail: The nation's parents were outraged and Topps withdrew the series. Years later Len Brown, who co-created *Mars Attacks!* with the late Woody Gelman, still laughs at the irony. The previous year the duo had concocted a card set marking the Civil War centennial that featured a blood-and-guts view of the historic conflict—plenty of slashing swords and disemboweling bayonets—and earned critical accolades, even the thanks of educators grateful to Topps for helping the nation's students learn their history.

Brown did enjoy a measure of revenge when *Mars Attacks!* was adapted in 1996 as a major Warner Brothers motion picture with all the trimmings—direction by acclaimed director Tim Burton, a big-league budget, an all-star cast, and rampaging Martians created by the computer graphics artists at the high-powered Industrial Light & Magic visual effects facility.

But morphing a garish sixties-era trading card creation into a big-screen spectacle in the nineties was just part of the transmogrification of popular culture. Brown recalls how back in the sixties, something like *Mars Attacks!* was total cult stuff. In fact, his old friend and boss Woody Gelman used the term "Third Eyes" to describe the then-underground nature of popular culture.

"Back in the early sixties fandom was much smaller," Brown recalls. "There were no comics collector's shops, fanzines were just beginning. Woody felt that the people who were interested in comics art, science fiction movies and TV, the old-time pulps and radio and such, were part of a kind of subculture. They had almost a Third Eye to see things the average person couldn't see."

LOST IN SPACE: *THE TRADING CARDS*

In the midsixties the nonsports cards produced by Brooklyn-based Topps ranged from Beatles cards to TV tie-ins like *Lost in Space*. Len Brown, who wrote the backs of the *Lost* card series, notes that while the show was filmed on the Fox lot in Hollywood, his still photo source was the network headquarters in Manhattan. "I remember going up to the 'Black Tower,' which is what we called the CBS Building here on Sixth Avenue. That's where they kept the

Not all science fiction fantasies were fuzzy, feel-good celebrations of the Wonder of it all: The nation's parents rose en masse to force Topps to withdraw its gory Mars Attacks! *card series (which, of course, was considered totally cool by kids). After suffering seemingly unending horrors from the Martian invaders, the Earthlings returned the favor by piloting spaceships to Mars "with revenge in their hearts." ©The Topps Company, Inc. From 1994 Deluxe Reissue.*

TELL A VISION

The cover of the May 7, 1945, issue of *Time* magazine is one of the most striking in that magazine's long history—an illustrated head shot of Adolf Hitler, Germany's Fuhrer, with a blood-red X slashed across his face. At that writing it wasn't known whether Hitler was dead or alive (he and his longtime mistress and death-pact wife had in fact committed suicide, the loyal aides who'd remained in the official bunker setting the corpses on fire), but it was clear that the Third Reich was collapsing under the ferocity of the Allied offensive.

That week's *Time* is a little time capsule of the mood of a nation nearing the end of World War II. A Caterpillar tractor ad in the magazine titled "Pattern for Tomorrow" promised to build super roads—"the highways of the future"—noting that one simple domestic dream had helped the American soldier tough out his death-defying duty: "He wants to get in his car and go." Even the Universal Camera Corporation proclaimed it had been providing valuable binoculars and other optical equipment for war ("eyes that seek out the enemy, find him . . . help to destroy him") and when "the war job is done" would be producing a new generation of camera and home movie equipment.

But one of the most interesting pieces in this 1945 *Time* is a two-page "Progress Report by RCA" titled "When Can You Expect Television?" The company promised that television able to broadcast "portrait quality pictures, almost as large as a newspaper page" would become a postwar reality. The medium was ready to go, with 118 television stations nationwide having applied to the Federal Communications Commission.

Referring to television as "radio's new 'dimension,'" RCA was confident that television would prove a golden boon for postwar America. Not only would the new commercial medium itself provide jobs, but the use of adver-

Time art by Boris Artzybasheff

tising would help create "such far-reaching stimulation of public buying that thousands upon thousands of additional workers will be needed to keep America's outlets and markets supplied."

The late-forties-through-fifties era of television has been called the medium's Golden Age. Special effects artist Jim Danforth had started out in the business during this seminal era, working with Art Clokey (the man who created Gumby) on a variety of TV projects. One assignment was producing special sequences and titles for NBC's *Dinah Shore Chevy Show*, one of the earliest variety programs and a color show as well (although you'd need an expensive color set to appreciate it).

"TV in the fifties was challenging and new," Danforth recalls. "What was exciting about the *Dinah Shore Chevy Show* was it was live and all-color at a time when most programs were black-and-white. NBC began having 'color spectaculars' where they'd do all-color original productions commissioned especially for television, such as a version of *Peter Pan* or *Cinderella*. For those spectaculars they'd write new songs and mount quite lavish productions.

"Once, for the *Dinah Shore Show*, they wanted to open the show with an Easter rabbit painting a blue egg on an easel. Matted in the egg would be the faces of the stars and guests for the show. Now, they had a process called chroma-key which preceded the various techniques we have now [for compositing separate visual elements into a single image]. You photographed your actors in front of blue and you replaced that blue with whatever background you wanted. But for this scene they wanted to do a reverse of that, with the rabbit painting an egg blue that shows the faces of Dinah and her guests. I pointed out we'd never done a chroma-key shot where the blue was on film. Could they pull a pure enough signal from the film to get the blue chroma-key system to work? It's different taking the RGB [red-green-blue] information right out of the camera when you're photographing the blue on the live stage with a live camera. So Art Clokey got on the phone to the NBC engineers and they agreed they'd better test it first. They found they could do it. That was a very minor thing, but even the simplest things were firsts in those days."

It was the stuff of miracles when a vaudeville crowd saw a pretty girl sing a song—even though she was in a studio a mile away. The stage screen's flickering image of the songstress was merely the latest advance in "radio television." This 1930 Popular Science *illustration explains the remarkable developments.*

A decade later television would become an all-color medium, with *Lost in Space* debuting in black-and-white and then being transformed into "living color." But while TV had moved beyond being "radio's new dimension," the medium had still not quite shaken its status as a kind of exotic furniture:

"Now, you don't have to decide which piece of furniture moves out when you move Color TV in," went the copy for a 1966 Zenith print ad. "Because now Zenith brings you a giant 25" Color picture-shaped like a movie screen—in new fine-furniture cabinets that are far trimmer, far slimmer than ordinary color consoles."

As the Space Race heated up, the pop cultural landscape reflected space adventuring themes, as seen in these comic book covers.

Lost in Space photo files. I'd go through the files and select the images for the cards. I always tried to get as many images of monsters as possible, because we felt kids really liked creatures."

Those were the days of relatively low-key licensing deals. The merchandising breakthrough of *Star Wars* was still more than a decade away, with additional decades to get to the high-powered reality of nineties pop culture properties capable of hundreds—even thousands—of product tie-ins. Brown's account of the peculiar hassles connected with an *Outer Limits* TV tie-in series would simply be unthinkable today.

"We didn't directly license the rights to do *Outer Limits* cards from the studio but from a licensing firm that told us the studio didn't have the right to license the original scripts," Brown recalls.

"They said they could give us the photos from the various episodes of the show, but the story on the back side of the card couldn't have anything to do with the actual episode! Since I wrote the backs, I'd have to make up almost ludicrous plots. It's almost embarrassing to reread them today. Other than the images, they had no connection with the actual shows! Today the licenser wouldn't stand for it.

"We didn't have that big a problem with *Lost in Space*, probably because it wasn't an anthology like *Outer Limits*, but a continuing series. *Lost in Space* shows were complete by themselves."

THE MAGICAL MUSEUM

In the past the artifacts of popular culture were considered disposable, even by the creators and companies. Tales are told of comics publishers bundling up and tossing into the fire reams of pages of original art, animation studios wiping celluloid-painted images clean or selling them for pocket change, movie studios auctioning off entire prop departments. Today, valuable movie memorabilia decorates the walls of Hollywood theme restaurants or is sold at big-ticket auctions, animation art is the stuff of books and museum exhibitions, and most studios have archival departments dedicated to preserving their creative artifacts. In short, what was once thrown away is now considered a corporate asset.

Jim Danforth, a veteran visual effects artist whose work includes such features as *The Wonderful World of the Brothers Grimm* (1962) and *When Dinosaurs Ruled the Earth* (1970), was part of the creative team that worked on such sixties TV programs as *The Outer Limits* and *Star Trek*. "I

Thousands of items of classic movie and TV fantasy production memorabilia crowd Bob Burns's magical museum in Burbank. Photos by Bruce Walters.

worked on the original *Star Trek* pilot, producing some of the original communicators the crew used—of course, if I'd known how big a hit that show was going to be, I'd have probably stuck a few away in my work box for future collectors," Danforth laughs. "But back then those shows were just another job. We'd get the blueprints for a prop from the art department and do the work. Sometimes we were allowed a little latitude. Of course, some people had a lot of dedication to what they were doing. Others looked down their noses at what they were doing, but that doesn't mean they still didn't do a good job."

In those days it was left to the Third Eye cult to appreciate the work of pros like Danforth, to value the mystical thrill of holding a real prop that had appeared on the movie screen or a TV program. Our friend Bob Burns, growing up in Burbank and in the very backyard of the Hollywood entertainment business, heard the siren call of the Third Eye. In 1948, his thirteenth year, he began a lifelong passion for collecting the stuff that dreams are made of when he came into possession of his first movie prop—the wolf's-head knob from the cane Claude Rains used to bludgeon the werewolf in the 1941 Universal classic *The Wolf Man*.

The plastic prop (which in the movie was supposed to be silver) had for years sat on a shelf in the shop of a movie prop maker named Ellis Burman, the father of one of Burns's schoolmates. "His studio was about four blocks from my home," Burns recalls, "and after school I'd visit and watch him make his props. I used to play with this wolf's head and one day he just gave it to me! This cane is featured throughout the movie and to actually be holding it in my hands—it was like the Holy Grail! Had I just thrown it away I'd be a normal person today."

Burns's collection today numbers some 2,500 artifacts. To house it all he had to add on a 3,000-square-foot museum to his Burbank home. The

wonders therein include the skeletal armature form of the original King Kong stop-motion puppet from 1933, a nine-foot spaceship from *Conquest of Space*, a seven-foot flying saucer used in *The Day the Earth Stood Still*, and a thirteen-foot-long backing of the moon's landscape painted by astronomical artist Chesley Bonestell that provided the first lunar view for the space crew of *Destination Moon*. But perhaps the most wonderful object in this pantheon of iconic artifacts is the vehicle that once whisked a man through dimensions of space and time—the Time Machine.

A TALE OF THE TIME MACHINE

The movie posters for George Pal's 1960 MGM release *The Time Machine* announced: "You will orbit into the Fantastic Future." Based on the seminal H. G. Wells science fiction novel, the production featured star Rod Taylor fast-forwarding from the Victorian age to the year 802,701, a time when docile, surface-dwelling Eloi are raised like cattle for the rapacious, subterranean Morlocks.

The machine that transported the hero and story forward was constructed of metal, wood, and plastic and stood some seven to eight feet long and almost five feet wide. The Time Machine's open carriage, with a barber's chair for a seat, featured a nearly seven-foot-tall dish that would spin as the time traveler began to accelerate through the years. George Pal had given a starstruck Burns the blueprints for the full-scale machine along with a prophecy: "George Pal once told me, 'Bob, someday you're going to end up with the machine. I know you will.' At the time he didn't even know what had happened to the prop, but he was very serious I'd end up with it. He was such a positive-thinking person. George felt there was always hope."

Years after the movie was released, Burns made a stab for the original Time Machine prop at a 1970 MGM auction. He'd come prepared to spend $1,000 but was crestfallen when the final bid topped off at $10,000 and the wonderful machine went to a showman who planned to exhibit the motion picture artifact in a traveling show.

Undaunted, Burns kept feelers out about the machine's whereabouts. He eventually heard that the traveling showman had run into financial trouble and had sold the machine. There had been rumors as to its whereabouts, but no one, not even Pal, knew what had become of the Time Machine. Five years slipped by without any news. It was as if the Time Machine had vanished into that impossible future.

"I guess it was fate, but one day in 1976, this guy was in an antique thrift shop in Orange, California, looking for movie props," Burns recalls. "In the back of this shop he saw the dish of the Time Machine! He called this friend of mine and told him about it. My friend called me and we were standing in that store within two hours. The chair was missing, the thrift shop owner having sold it because he thought it was an antique barber's chair. Glass pods on the prop had been broken. The guy hadn't taken care of it at all. He didn't even know what it was, just that it'd been in some famous movie. It was just a white elephant for him because he'd only gotten it to sell the barber's chair. He thought it was a real antique chair. But if whoever owns that chair turns it upside down they'll see a note saying 'MGM Prop Department.'"

After a tense, cagey negotiation, Burns finally handed over the thousand bucks that had been burning a hole in his pocket and took possession of the Time Machine. He first stored it in his garage in Burbank and, using the original movie blueprints he'd gotten from Pal years before, began to have a new chair constructed to the original's exacting specifications. Any broken pieces were repaired, any tarnish polished to a gleam.

Halloween was coming up, and Burns and some of his fellow movie effects artists had an annual tradition of free outdoor illusion shows held

In Bob Burns's magical museum, the author contemplates a ride in the Time Machine, the original prop from the George Pal movie. (Note, on the back wall, a section of lunar landscape—with Earth in the heavens—created by Chesley Bonestell for Destination Moon.) *Photo by Bruce Walters.*

on a raised stage on the grounds of Burns's Burbank home. It was appropriate, given that it was the national Bicentennial, that the wonderful Time Machine would be the centerpiece of that year's Halloween illusion show. With the Hollywood effects artists working their magic, the crowds for the various performances thrilled as a time traveler again sat at the Time controls. Once again the venerable device began to hum, and the audiences witnessed the voyager magically transported from the Victorian comforts of a nineteenth-century mansion to the future age of Eloi and Morlocks.

"I remember when I first got the Machine I was so excited," Burns happily recalls. "I called George Pal and I said, 'George, you're not going to believe this—I actually found the Time Machine!' There was this pause and then George goes, 'Of course. I told you that you were going to get it.' And then he started laughing! He thought it was the most wonderful thing in the world."

THE KINGDOM OF SUNDAY NIGHT

After 23 years and 1,087 hours of live television, you'd have expected it to go out with a really, **really** *big show. Instead,* **The Ed Sullivan Show** *ended on a strangely anticlimactic note. A rerun from four months earlier. . . .*

—*"THE LAST REALLY BIG SHOW," BY A. J. JACOBS,* ENTERTAINMENT WEEKLY, *JUNE 7, 1996*

Television in 1997 is almost a different medium from the era of the *Lost in Space* series. Today, miniature home satellite dishes can pick up hundreds of channels, giant cable networks provide twenty-four-hour specialty programming on everything from news to sports, and videocassette recorders allow viewers the freedom of taping programs for later viewing or popping in alternative programming altogether.

But back in 1965 a viewer had to be in front of the set to catch a program, and once it was broadcast it was gone, just more electromagnetic waves heading out into space. Only three network channels broadcast nationally—ABC, CBS, and NBC—complemented by local affiliates and a public station or two. It was an era when mass audiences could simultaneously view the same live entertainment programs and unfolding historical events. (In the aftermath of President Kennedy's assassination in 1963, many shocked TV viewers saw accused assassin Lee Harvey Oswald shot by Jack Ruby, while the entire nation watched broadcasts of the funeral procession and shared in the mourning.)

One of the most popular shows of the era, and a Sunday night tradition for almost a quarter-century, was *The Ed Sullivan Show*. Sullivan himself became legendary for his wooden personality—comedian Jack Carter reportedly called the program "the only live show with a dead host." But somehow the *Sullivan* variety show was the destination for the megatalent of the time, resulting in such historic programs as the February 9, 1964, show that introduced the Beatles to the U.S. and generated the largest viewing audience in history up to that point.

Vince Calandra, who joined the *Sullivan* show in the late fifties as a "cue card guy" and in 1961 graduated to production assistant, became the show's talent executive by 1964 (in time to book the Beatles for that historic show). Although the *Sullivan* show was canceled in 1971, Calandra has never stopped working, his career stretching from talent executive work on *The Mike Douglas Show* to producing HBO specials and today doing the talent honors for the *Home & Family* show on the Family Channel.

But for Calandra, *The Ed Sullivan Show* represents a golden time. He was a young man working in New York and rubbing elbows with the most famous people on earth. Every door opened, the best tables waited at the hottest nightclubs, and a single phone call could connect him with the rich and powerful. Energywise, it was a Happy Hour without the hangover, a party that seemingly would never end.

TV in the midsixties was itself still young, and truly the electronic hearth . . .

You cannot comprehend the excitement of going to work every week. That was it! My God, unbelievable. We'd do the show live from New York every Sunday, eight to nine. I was also going out to the clubs like six nights a week to see people and acts. The Copacabana, the Americana Hotel, the Paramount, Basin Street East, all these clubs that are now all gone. I saw everything on Broadway and off-Broadway. I'd also just gotten married [in 1960] and I had my first kid. It was like burnout time. Lots of pressure week to week. I was getting an ulcer. But I didn't grasp the situation at the time. There was so much I still could have seen and learned. That's what amazes me. I'm still learning at the age of sixty-three.

Most of the descriptions of Ed Sullivan are accurate, but I saw a side of him that people never saw. He was a street guy and I was a street guy. I was brought up in Brooklyn in a four-room railroad apartment by grandparents who only spoke Sicilian. When I got work on the **Sullivan** show and they'd need somebody to travel with the old man it'd be like, 'Oh God, we've got to have the kid Vince travel with Sullivan again.' But I loved that! Ed liked me because I could talk to him. I mean, I was a kid from Brooklyn, what was I going to do growing up? I read baseball and football books—all that stuff was right up his alley, because Ed's background was as a sportswriter.

Ed had a feeling for what an audience wanted. He was also very loyal to old vaudeville people and athletes who were kind to him when he was a sportswriter struggling in New York. It was a cardinal rule that I had to book some of these old people all the time on the show. We couldn't understand why until we realized that to keep up their health benefits with the union [the American Federation of Television Artists] they had to make a certain number of television appearances. So they'd come on and we'd make them feel like they were still stars. That's how I learned to survive for thirty-eight years—I was always told to be respectful. Not that I hadn't been brought up that way, but you just never know. It's a very small business and word gets around very fast.

I was in awe of Ed Sullivan. Sinatra. Joe DiMaggio. Kirk Douglas was like my idol. The first time I met Douglas I shook his hand. "Mr. Douglas, a pleasure to meet you." And he replies, "Hey kid, where can I take a piss?" But I'm good on the talent end because I know when the act wants to talk and when the act doesn't want to be bothered. "Can I get you a cup of coffee? Nice to see you, thanks for coming." And I'm gone.

I'd book months ahead. It was easy. We'd sit with the agents from the three major agencies and we'd go, "Yeah, Tony Bennett—six shots." Boom-boom-boom. We dealt with the agents because that was their big ten percent, man. Then for the typical Sullivan week we'd go in for a Tuesday production meeting to discuss who was going to be on that week's show. If there was going to be a production number we'd rehearse it Wednesday through Friday. We'd block the show on Saturday. Then on Sunday we'd do a dress rehearsal at two o'clock in the afternoon and then go on live that evening.

We'd sometimes go on remotes and we were required to wear shirt and tie. Now I do shows where people go on in warm-up suits and tennis shoes. When the Berlin Wall was being built we were one of the few shows to go over and do a show there. When we flew in and out of Berlin we were followed by reconnaissance planes.

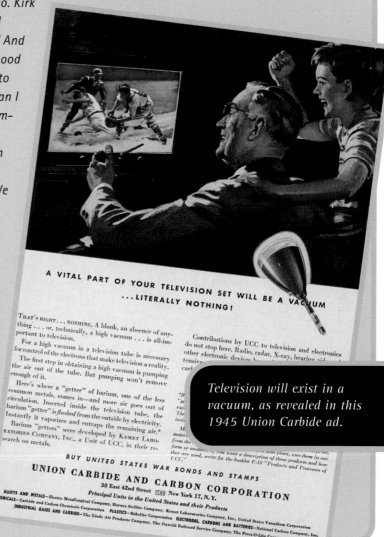

Television will exist in a vacuum, as revealed in this 1945 Union Carbide ad.

In addition to the Beatles' appearance on the **Sullivan** show, we also produced their concert at Shea Stadium. By then, our crew had been working together about six or seven years. We put that Shea show together in three days, something ridiculous like that, complete with sixteen cameras covering it. The funny thing is, there was never a copyright on that show! It was an ABC program that Brian [Epstein, the Beatles' manager] hired us to produce for them.

Ed introduced them, just saying, "Here are the Beatles." Of course, you couldn't even hear him say that. My God, it was so loud with the audience just screaming through the whole thing. If you look at a tape of that show at one point you'll see Paul McCartney and John Lennon just laughing at each other. What happened was John was playing one song and Paul was singing another, that's how loud it was. Years later I realized what a schmuck I was because in the dugout and the visiting clubhouse they'd left so much signed stuff they didn't want to take home or be bothered with. Paul had written the songs for the show on the back of a Mets scorecard—and me not keeping it! I'm tellin' ya. I was also good friends with their roadie who had all this stuff, a kid from Liverpool, a boyhood friend of the guys who unfortunately got into very heavy drugs and got blown away by the LAPD ten years ago.

The Beatles were just amazed at the reaction they got, the screaming and all that. Ringo told me, "You Americans are goddamned crazy!" How could people react this way? Believe me, we had no idea. It was just in '63 that George Harrison had come to Minneapolis to visit his sister who lived there. The Beatles were then number-one in Europe but he went to a Minneapolis record store and could not find one of their records! Back in Liverpool he told the guys they were like zero back in the States. But then a disc jockey in Washington, D.C., asked an airline stewardess to bring back from England this Beatles record "I Want to Hold Your Hand." He played it for twelve or twenty-four straight hours and that's what started the whole wave.

Actually, people today claim the reason the Beatles happened was because after the assassination of President Kennedy people were looking for something to make them happy. There was Haight-Ashbury, the Fifth Dimension and all that real "up" music, the Motown sound.

We rolled the dice with a lot of the rock acts because we were live, there was no delay. In the early sixties we canceled Bob Dylan because he was going to do a protest song and he wouldn't change the lyrics. There was another famous incident where we wanted the Stones to change the song "Let's Spend the Night Together" to "Let's Spend Some Time Together." I was one of the people who asked Mick Jagger to change the lyric. He told me to get the fuck off the stage [Jagger did incorporate the change].

At the Ed Sullivan theater we had this little green room in the back and once we had a meeting there with Jimi Hendrix to discuss having him on the show. And one of the things we discussed was the idea of having a big special built around Rudolf Nureyev dancing to a Hendrix composition. Nureyev had already said he would do it. And we had Hendrix. It was a done deal. Then Hendrix goes and OD's two weeks later in London. That was something great we never did.

I remember when the **Sullivan** show was canceled in 1971. Unfortunately the last time I saw Sullivan after that was at his funeral [in 1974]. But I'll tell you exactly how it went down the last time I was with him. We were in the editing room on a Thursday and Bob Precht, our producer, got a call from the vice president of CBS television telling him that the show was not being renewed. So Bob called Ed right away so he'd hear it before the news people. And Sullivan says, "Those sons-of-bitches. You'd think they'd give me twenty-five years. All the goddamn money I made for that fucking network. That's it. It's over." We never did a farewell show. We just went off. He was bitter! He wanted to do twenty-five years. He was very big into the loyalty thing.

On the **Sullivan** show we'd have Streisand and Red Skelton on the same show with the Rolling Stones. It was like a Who's Who every week. I look at tapes of those shows and I think, "My God, this is really classy." When I did talent for Sullivan and Mike Douglas no one ever said 'No' to me. I could get things done with one phone call. But today I can't put together the combinations I once did.

I was recently trying to book five different stars from a movie and I had to call five different agents. Even getting on a press junket nowadays requires having to be approved by the movie company, then a PR person who then finally shows it to the star. But still, the new era of television is incredible, with the editing alone—it used to take us hours and hours in the editing room just slicing tape together.

But you know what really amazes me today? You want to talk about culture shock. Back when we had the Beatles on we were getting letters from clergy: "How could you?" And here were four clean-cut guys in suits but with moptop haircuts that would be nothing today. Now I see these talk shows that have topics like lesbian nuns or "I want to sleep with my mother"—and those ratings are going through the roof! Well, if that's what television is going to be like, then forget about it. But you know something? If I can't sleep at night I'll put on those shows. It's so ridiculous. But I sit there and watch it!

It's just a whole different era. Today we're so saturated with all the media. To me it's like the expansion of Major League Baseball, where things get watered down. I really wish I'd been a young man during the Godfather years in the forties and fifties. That's the era I really loved. I could have fit in New York with that Art Deco style, double-breasted suits, and flashy convertibles. Like Al Pacino in **The Godfather**. Maybe I should have been a Mafia Don—I missed my calling! [laughs]

Irwin Allen (CENTER), *and star Paul Newman* (FAR RIGHT), *discuss a Joe Musso* Towering Inferno *story-board sequence as Joe looks on.*

③ THE PRODUCER

> *If I can't blow up the world within the first ten minutes, then the show is a flop.*
>
> —IRWIN ALLEN, QUOTED IN FANTASTIC TELEVISION, 1977
>
> *Structurally* Independence Day *is an homage to the Irwin Allen disaster films of the seventies, where a lot of characters are drawn together by a cataclysmic event.*
>
> —DEAN DEVLIN, PRODUCER OF INDEPENDENCE DAY, QUOTED IN CINEFEX #67, SEPTEMBER 1996

Producer/director Irwin Allen essentially had two professional lives: His run as the golden boy of Twentieth Century Fox's television unit during the 1960s (producing not only *Lost in Space* but *Voyage to the Bottom of the Sea*, *The Time Tunnel*, and *Land of the Giants*) and his reign as the "Master of Disaster" who brought to the big screen such seventies blockbuster spectacles as *The Poseidon Adventure* and *The Towering Inferno*.

Born in New York City on June 12, 1916, Allen's love of entertainment started with the "thrill rides" of Coney Island. As an adult he would craft his own thrill rides in the movie medium, but his professional career also included being an Oscar-winning documentarian and a traditionalist who loved family values (a quality he celebrated in *Lost in Space*). Even as a grown man he never lost his childlike love for the circus. In many ways he was like a big kid.

"He was living his childhood," says Joe Musso, smiling, a veteran movie concept artist who began his own career, and a long association with Allen, on *Towering Inferno*. "He had a prop maker to make production models who was basically making toys for Irwin. He made the kinds of films he'd want to see if he was a kid going to the movies.

"When Irwin first came to California in the forties, he got work at the Orsatti talent agency, and he had a table in his office crowded with windup toys," Musso adds. "He'd be in there with producers putting deals together and somehow things always got around to these windup toys. He'd start winding them up and pretty soon everybody would be playing with these toys! Eventually he started to sell himself with the projects."

THE FRUGAL PRODUCER

Allen's earliest breakthrough was acquiring the rights to Rachel Carson's bestselling book *The Sea Around Us*. The resulting underwater documentary was released through RKO Radio Pictures (the famed studio that had produced such classics as *King Kong* and *Citizen Kane*). As the film's theatrical trailer voice-over narration exclaimed: "From all the seven seas around the world, from 100 ports of call, comes the exciting drama of a thrilling world of wonders you've never seen before: *The Sea Around Us*!"

The underwater documentary evinced not only showmanship but the savvy showbiz acumen that would take the ambitious producer to the top. "Irwin convinced RKO that they could put *The Sea Around Us* together using stock footage and that

Irwin Allen was a man of big dreams, one of which was a "Pleasure Island" amusement park. The dream never came to fruition, but this mock-up (featuring the beloved Seaview submarine from Voyage to the Bottom of the Sea*) is a rare artifact from the Pleasure Island concept stage. (From the collection of Bob Burns; photo by Bruce Walters.)*

Allen's *The Time Tunnel* TV show had two scientists landing in a different time zone in each week's episode (essentially combining H. G. Wells's *The Time Machine* with the premise of *Lost in Space*), and was pitched to the studio as a stock-footage dream. "Irwin went to Fox and sold them on *Time Tunnel* by pointing out the studio had made all these epic historical films with all this stock footage," Musso says. "In this series they could go back and forth in time reusing all this footage. That's exactly what they did. The first episode had the time travelers landing on the *Titanic*. Fox had released a black-and-white film on the *Titanic* in the early fifties, so they used some of that footage as kind of a montage, loosely tinted, on that episode."

ALLEN'S FOX TV UNIT

Musso recalls that during the sixties Allen became "the fair-haired boy" on the Fox lot, one of the big producers for the studio's television unit. "His office at Fox was like a war room," says Roy Alexander, who joined Allen as a concept artist on *Lost in Space*. "One entire wall was filled with graphs charting all the various production activity on each series he had working. I remember that was

it'd be a shoe-in to win the Academy Award for best documentary," Musso remembers. "So he wrote to all the nautical labs and universities regarding any footage they had on underwater life, they culled through it all, and put together the documentary. And it won the 1952 Academy Award, just as Irwin predicted. From that point on Irwin never looked back as a producer."

Allen wasn't loathe to spend big bucks for big effects. For his 1961 film *Voyage to the Bottom of the Sea* (released through Twentieth Century Fox), the producer/director spent the then considerable sum of $400,000 for a lavish set of the *Seaview* supersubmarine, complete from control room to torpedo bays. The *Lost in Space* TV pilot cost a then unprecedented $700,000. But Allen also never saw a prop he couldn't reuse. For example, that *Seaview* movie set, and even footage from the film, would be used in the *Voyage* TV series, which debuted on ABC in 1964.

"The Derelict," Lost in Space*'s second episode, elicited this "CBS Requests" memo asking that the role of Dr. Smith be emphasized—and that "the sweetness and light" be reviewed and eliminated. (Document made available through the courtesy of the University of California at Los Angeles Arts Library–Special Collections.)*

EPISODE #2

a) Re-establish Smith's function and mission and the fact that he was an interloper.

b) Carefully review and eliminate all the sweetness and light. Also, double check objectionable lines indicated in marked script. (Especially watch stage directions indicating such attitude in order that the director not be misled.

c) Smith's speech in the middle of Page 22 should have the addition "and get back to earth".

d) John's voice - Scene 101 - speech should comment on the presence of Smith and the annoyance he has caused the family.

e) Re the "bubble people" - sound effects will play an important part here - use echo chambers -- to get humanistic aspect to a non-human looking apparition. Have Will remark "they are not like us but maybe they are".

f) Page 58 - Scene 234 - John's first speech, change the word alien to inhuman.

one of the things we hated doing, going in and updating Irwin's charts for him. He thought big!"

Allen's rise to prominence had come at a time when the movies had finally embraced the television medium. During the previous decade the studios had been forced by court decrees to divest themselves of the nationwide theater chains they had owned for years. The loss of guaranteed income, plus the competition from the new TV medium and the financial drain from blockbuster cost overruns (such as Fox's own 1963 release *Cleopatra*, at $37 million the most expensive movie ever made to that point), meant the studios had been operating at a loss for years.

"In the seventies, Bank of America, which was largely involved in loaning production money, did an analysis that found that in the aggregate the Hollywood studios when averaged out had been operating at a loss for the previous twenty years," Jim Danforth recalls. "The only reason they were still in business was they'd begun selling off their assets, such as their effects and prop departments, back lots, and so on. You know, when you sell off the back lot that becomes Century City you pay for the losses on *Cleopatra*—which had run Twentieth Century Fox into poverty! To cover their losses they were even pumping oil on the Fox lot. You could see these derricks covered in tar paper and canvas."

On the Fox lot Allen was a no-nonsense, hard-driving producer. Ned Gorman, a visual effects producer at Industrial Light & Magic, recalls being on a panel in the midnineties with a unit production manager from Allen's *Lost in Space* days, a fellow who related an incident that summed up Allen's no-nonsense nature.

"They were shooting a *Lost in Space* episode and they had a director who was evidently having a vision about the episode," Gorman relates. "Allen had a strict no-overtime rule in place, so you weren't supposed to shoot past six o'clock. It didn't matter if Jesus was descending from heaven, you

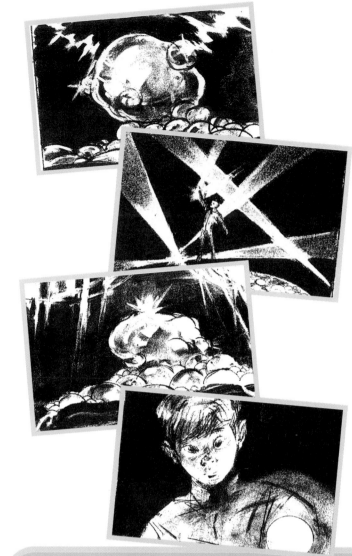

In "The Derelict," the wandering Jupiter 2 crew enter another lost spacecraft and encounter alien "bubble creatures." This storyboard sequence plots out Will Robinson's encounter with the strange creatures.
(Art made available through the courtesy of the University of California at Los Angeles Arts Library–Special Collections.)

didn't shoot past six o'clock. This particular director wasn't going to get all his setups for the day, so the unit production manager goes up to Allen's office and tells him the guy's going to go past six o'clock. And Allen is like, what are you bothering me with this for? You don't shoot past six o'clock. 'How do I stop him?' he asks Allen. And Allen tells him to go down and at six o'clock just walk up to the camera and put his hand in front of the lens. So the guy

ALLEN'S INFERNO

I will count one-two-three and somewhere on the way to ten a pistol shot will go off and within two seconds after that the big explosion will occur.

—IRWIN ALLEN BRACING HIS CREW AND ACTORS (WITH BLANK-SHOOTING PISTOL IN HAND) PRIOR TO CALLING "ACTION" ON FILMING THE EXPLOSIVE TOWERING INFERNO *FINALE*

The professional apex for Irwin Allen was his production *The Towering Inferno*, for which he also directed the many action sequences (with John Guillermin credited as overall director). The disaster picture formula was a matter of throwing a bunch of people into some elemental fury and then watching things play out through life-and-death situations. The cowards would show their true colors and the heroes their strength and bravery. It was simple and straightforward—and the stuff of blockbusters.

The setup for *Inferno* had a glass super-skyscraper in San Francisco catching fire—sparked by the bad electrical wiring installed by unscrupulous developers—and trapping hundreds of wealthy and powerful celebrants during the gala opening night festivities. The all-star cast featured Paul Newman as the "Architect," William Holden as the "Builder," and Steve McQueen as the daring "Fireman," and also included Faye Dunaway, Fred Astaire, Jennifer Jones, Richard Wagner, and O. J. Simpson.

Artist Joe Musso, an ex-Marine who in the early seventies had come to California with his portfolio hoping to do concept artwork for "somebody like Cecil B. DeMille," got his wish when Irwin Allen looked at his work and hired him on the spot. "On one of our first production meetings for *Towering Inferno* Irwin said, 'We're here to prove the *Poseidon Adventure* wasn't a mistake and we can do it again,'" Musso remembers. "What he wanted in *Towering Inferno* was for each action sequence to be slightly more spectacular than the one that preceded it. He wanted it to build and build. And he orchestrated it magnificently. As a matter of fact, actors like Paul Newman and Bill Holden, when they're through with their scenes, will usually get away from a set. Well, in this movie everybody was so excited they just hung around the set. It was spectacular watching this whole thing happen. Nobody wanted to miss anything."

The skyscraper itself was conceived as some 1,040 feet tall, by Joe Musso's estimates. "Just to get it straight in our own minds, we had the entire geography of the skyscraper figured out—where all the floors were and where fires would break out," Musso notes. "We knew where Fred Astaire's room was, where the stairwell was where Paul Newman encounters an explosion, where Steve McQueen's character had his headquarters—everything about the building."

The production had four different units—a first unit for all the dramatic scenes, an action unit with its own camera crew, a special effects miniatures unit headed up by L. B. Abbott (another Allen veteran, who had provided the visual effects for most of Allen's previous TV productions, including *Lost in Space*), and a San Francisco unit for ground-level and aerial footage. This film is recalled by many of the cast and crew as being exemplary of Allen's superb preparations. Despite the physical fire effects, the many stunts, even the fantastic finale featuring pyrotechnics and a torrent of water dousing many of the stars, no one was seriously injured during the production.

Musso worked simultaneously on storyboard and concept art for all four camera units, such as a spectacular sequence in which an explosion causes an outside elevator to hang perilously from the side of the flaming skyscraper. That sequence had to cut together separately shot exterior tower views, including cuts from a soundstage elevator set complete with actors and backing; a four-story outdoor mock-up of the elevator and building facade for stunts (personally directed by Allen); aerial location footage; and the establishing shots created by Abbott's miniatures crew.

"Irwin always wanted his people to dream up ideas," Musso says. "For example, in the original script Paul Newman somehow gets separated from Jennifer Jones's character and the two children who are with her, so he tosses a fire hose to them so they can climb down. But at a meeting Irwin said he didn't want to do it that way. A similar gag had been done in the *Poseidon Adventure* and he heard this new film *Earthquake* was going to do something like it. So how else could we do it? I suggested he have Newman walking ahead down the stairwell when an explosion causes the staircase to drop two floors, with the woman and kids trapped above. He thought that was wonderful, but how were they going to get down? I said that they could climb down on this length of twisted wrought-iron stairwell. 'You got an idea of how that's going to look?' he asks. I told him yes. 'Draw it up,' he says, 'we'll film it.' Basically Irwin let me write this whole sequence."

In retrospect, *Towering Inferno* was probably the last blockbuster of the post-studio era of Hollywood. The following year a young director named Steven Spielberg would release *Jaws* and in 1977 *Star Wars* would usher in the modern era of high-powered, digitally crafted visual effects films.

Musso, whose continuing career has stretched from work with director Alfred Hitchcock on *Torn Curtain* to 1997's Allenesque *Volcano*, affectionately remembers the producer as one of the last of the great Hollywood moguls. In trying to describe the producer's bombastic enthusiasm, Musso recalls the time he and fellow production artist Tom Cranham, preparing for concept work on the eventual 1978 killer bees thriller *Swarm*, suggested to Allen that since he favored big visual concept presentations, they could make slides of the concept art and project it on screens. That way Allen would have a five-by-eight-foot image to consider.

"Well, Irwin loved that idea so much that he got the bright idea that we start doing our concept sketches at five by eight feet!" Musso laughs. "We were making murals! They were so big we had to roll and unroll these lengths of paper and work in a corridor. Tom and I had to use spray cans filled with felt-tip ink to spray in big areas of bees attacking or an atom bomb explosion. The fumes were going everywhere. That lasted for a couple of sketches before we went back to the old way of doing things.

Custer's Charge at Hanover, *oil painting by Joe Musso for A & E network production*

"Irwin was a showman, pure and simple," Musso concludes. "He always thought big. He wanted visual spectacle and he hired the best people to get it on the screen. And if he could get something that had never been seen before, that was absolutely wonderful!"

goes back to the set, six o'clock comes up and the director is still rolling—and the guy walks up right in the middle of the take and puts his hand in front of the lens. So the director goes storming up to Allen's office and says what just happened. 'Yeah, that's what I told him to do,' Allen says. The director is blustering, he almost has a heart attack, and Allen tells him to just come back the next morning. I love that! Business is business."

From being the star of Fox's TV unit, Allen would permanently transcend to the silver screen side with the 1972 Fox release *The Poseidon Adventure* and 1974's *The Towering Inferno* (coreleased with Warner Brothers). "I remember when I was working on *The Towering Inferno* that it was one of those productions where I just realized—this is IT!" exults Joe Musso. "If somebody had a good idea he'd jump on it. But after *Inferno* Irwin became less receptive in some areas. He'd become so flush with success, and was now a superstar producer, so I guess he was afraid to show weakness by admitting a mistake or changing his mind. Then he came around and became his old self."

ALLEN'S CIRCUS

After his years with Fox, Allen eventually went over to Warner Brothers, where he was installed in grand style. "Irwin Allen was one of the top guys at Warner Brothers at the time," Danforth remembers. "It was like Steven Spielberg today. They built him this whole bungalow with a suite of offices."

One of the traditions Allen brought over to Warner's from Fox was an annual outing for studio executives and their families when the Ringling Brothers circus came to town. Allen would charter buses, decorating them with bunting and streamers, and hire circus clowns to ride along and entertain the kids and hand out balloons.

One of Allen's early movie productions had been his 1959 release *The Big Circus*, which featured real circus acts as well as an all-star cast that included Victor Mature, Rhonda Fleming, Vincent Price, and Peter Lorre. There was even a circus theme in the *Lost in Space* episode "Space Circus," which featured one Dr. Marvello putting on "The Greatest Show in Space" for the *Jupiter 2* company, a space-traveling show featuring a space monster, a juggler of "cosmic forces," and a mistress of psychic phenomena.

In fact, a circus movie was one of the big projects Allen had in development in the midseventies. Allen wanted to create the ultimate circus movie, bigger than Cecil B. DeMille's circus film *The Greatest Show on Earth*, bigger even than his own 1959 production. Allen dreamed of producing his new circus movie in conjunction with Ringling Brothers, with another all-star cast headed by Steve McQueen. But a script was never developed to complement the planned spectacle and effects. It was one of his dreams that never came to pass. "The enthusiasm was there, but maybe what became difficult for him was that things change," Musso muses. "The things you liked as a kid aren't necessarily the things the next generation is going to like."

TWILIGHT OF A CAREER

Allen's long, unbroken streak of success, a ride that lasted for more than two decades, finally hit a bumpy stretch. Warner's didn't renew his contract, and he moved over to Columbia. A live-action *Pinocchio* production, which would have been produced with Warner Brothers picking up half the costs, didn't make it out of preproduction when the other half of the funding fell through. A planned *Oh, God! 4*, the series vehicle for George Burns, collapsed when it was discovered the production couldn't obtain insurance to cover the elderly star. Allen even had on the drawing board plans for "Pleasure Island," an ambitious Hollywood-themed amusement park that likewise never achieved liftoff.

"One project after another seemed to collapse for reasons that had nothing to do with Irwin him-

Despite being lost in space, there was no escaping Allen's childlike love of classic Americana, as in these scenes of Smith and the Robot meeting a mechanical junk man of space (in "Junkyard of Space," the last show of the series) and Will and Smith encountering intergalactic showman Farnum B. (played by Leonard Stone in the third season episode "A Day at the Zoo").

self," says Musso. "Then he was starting to get a couple things going when all of a sudden his health began to fail him. But he was a ball of fire almost to the end."

While Allen was convalescing from heart and kidney troubles, Musso recalls being invited to visit his old friend and boss for lunch at the producer's Malibu home. Allen was looking forward to getting back to the studio. Musso has a vivid memory of Allen's wife gently remonstrating her husband for insisting on personally answering all his fan mail. Soon afterward, Musso received word that on November 2, 1991, Allen had died of a heart attack in Los Angeles. Left undone at Allen's death was not only the ultimate circus movie but a long-planned feature film version of Lost in Space.

Ironically, in the nineties Irwin Allen films would come back in vogue, with star-filled disaster

epics ranging from natural forces unleashed in such films as Twister and Volcano to the alien invasion motif of Independence Day. "One of the first things I said walking out of the theater after seeing Independence Day was, 'Irwin would be proud!'" laughs Ned Gorman.

LOST *EFFECTS*

October 16, 1997—This is the beginning. This is the day. You are watching the unfolding of one of man's great adventures. Man's colonization of space; beyond the stars.

—NARRATION ON LOST IN SPACE *PILOT*, 1965

In the sixties there was a kind of technological innocence, a sense of Space Age wonders still unfolding. Devotees of Third Eye culture were also at that nexus between imagination and reality. Even if one lived out in the middle of nowhere, a few nifty adjustments of the rabbit-ear antenna on the home set might draw in the transmissions emanating from the nearest, but distant, big-city TV station. Perhaps when the white snow and static cleared it'd reveal a midnight horror show, maybe a legendary movie unseen since its original theatrical release. And then the viewer would have to stay focused on the flickering screen, since there was no possibility of pausing or freeze-framing (the first "cassette TV," as *Life* magazine called it in an October 16, 1970, article, products wouldn't begin popping up in the marketplace until the early seventies). Of course, moviegoers also had to pay rapt attention in a movie theater, since once a picture had its run it might never be seen again.

Such was the mind-set when the *Lost in Space* TV show was in production. As Jim Danforth noted earlier, this was also the era when a show was "just another job" to effects artists faced with the pressures of conjuring up illusions on a weekly basis. While the *Lost* pilot was a big-budget affair, the nearly thirty episodes produced each season were achieved with more spartan allowances.

"Consider that in 1997 Jerry Seinfeld made a million dollars an episode—that might have been a whole season's budget for *Lost in Space*," laughs original series artist Roy Alexander. "I can't remember what the per-episode budget was, but a guest star would make $2,500 for one show—and we thought that was a lot of money then! There were budget constraints, so we couldn't do anything outrageously expensive. The effects stuff we did was pretty simple and straightforward. Of course, the limits of the effects back then was a given."

Alexander, along with Tom Cranham, George Jensen, and other concept artists, were vital in creating the illusion of a weekly sojourn into outer space. Their assignments ranged from storyboarding effects sequences (in the process working closely with effects head L. B. Abbott) to designing sets and the occasional prop, such as sidearms Tom Cranham designed for the second season that were produced by the Fox model shop. The creative process they followed is relatively unchanged today: The first step would be to read the script, breaking sequences into set pieces and effects, then work on the particular designs and camera compositions with the overall art director and the various production departments as needed. "On *Lost in Space* Tom, George, and I were new in the business and just starstruck by the whole thing," Alexander recalls. "Each week we saw the entire process of putting together a piece of filmed entertainment from the ground up."

Of course, the rookies were being ushered into the wonderful world of show business by the master, Irwin Allen. And one of the tricks of the trade was recycling as needed. "Bob Kinoshita [one of the show's art directors] called it 'stacking beer kegs,'" Cranham says, laughing. "Often in the script there'd be some weird mechanical thing that had to come rolling into the set, so the Fox lot would be scoured for things they could slam together, trick up, and wire, and which could be motorized or pulled by monofilament wires or whatever."

Sometimes the recycling backfired, detracting from, not enhancing, a production. "*Time Tunnel* seemed like it started out with a lot of promise," cites Cranham, "but instead of just doing a story about an interesting time period, every place they went had to be some epic historical event for which they could use stock footage. Irwin would sometimes try to put a square peg in a round hole, but we'd always give it a shot."

Planning the look and compositions of the effects sequences required creating detailed storyboards. "The idea of the storyboards, which were strictly black-and-white illustrations breaking down a particular sequence, was not only to explain what we wanted to see on film, but to make sure everybody involved with the production was on the same page," Cranham explains. "We might storyboard if it was an action sequence with stunt doubles, but mostly we boarded the effects. There was no point in storyboarding straight dialogue between the actors."

The design work also included planning sets for each episode. Designs ultimately approved by the art director would be passed to the set designers, who would physically realize the concept on the shooting stage. Some of the *Lost* episodes had spectacular sets, such as the labyrinthine ruins of an alien city that appeared in the first-season episode "There Were Giants in the Earth."

Many of the conjured-up environments utilized classic theatrical "limbo set" designs. "A limbo set is just a big black curtain around the area of the scene, so the background just disappears into darkness," Alexander explains. "We'd visualize something that would work that we could stick in there. For example, we had one story about a space pirate, so for that episode we designed a limbo set featuring the bridge of a pirate's ship, with the interior also utilizing a limbo set."

Since most of the *Lost* episodes revolved around the Robinsons' alien world settlement (whatever planet they might be on during a particular season or episode), a key production venue was the soundstage set featuring the full-scale *Jupiter 2* exterior. The alien locale surrounding the spaceship set piece was a set floor filled with sand, while the distant land masses, horizon, and sky involved painted set backings. Plaster rock formations dressing the set could also be moved and rearranged in another corner of the vast soundstage when it was necessary to depict characters venturing deeper into the alien environment.

The effects work included simple opticals (such as "split screens," in which a film frame is divided into segments containing a separate image), Abbott's saucer models flown by wires, pyrotechnic effects, painted translight backings depicting outer space or a particular alien landscape placed outside the *Jupiter 2* set view windows, and hand-drawn cel animation effects for everything from the laser gun blasts to the Robot's own discharges of electrical firepower. "If it was a ray gun fire we'd have to come up with a design look, such as a steady or a pulsating beam," Tom Cranham notes, "but we had to have enough lead time to do the different animation effects."

"There were always three or four, sometimes five, sketch artists working for Irwin, which was fairly unique in the TV business back then," Alexander adds. "Irwin had a contract with Fox that included a provision that the studio provide a sketch artist for each of his TV shows. His shows were fantasy, and visuals were important. Plus, Irwin couldn't visualize. He needed to see things. He would know what he wanted when he saw it.

"The thing that stands out for me about *Lost in Space* was it was my first job in the entertainment business," Alexander concludes. "The other thing is I made several of what have turned out to be lifelong friends. That's what makes it special to me."

While 1997 TV science fiction shows conjure up alien environments using computer graphics, fantasy fare in the Lost in Space *era did it the old-fashioned way—with sets, props, and painted backings.*

L IT'S A MAN'S UNIVERSE

In our alternate *Lost in Space* universe of 1997, there are no "gender issues," as someone today might put it—the man still rules. John Robinson was squarely in command of the *Jupiter 2*, followed by Don West, with the occasional alpha-male dustup between the two (in the midsixties it was still shocking to challenge one's commander-in-chief). Even young Will was higher in the pecking order than the womenfolk.

HELPLESS FEMALES

In the first-season episode "One of Our Dogs Is Missing," John and Don are off on a mission, leaving the females to guard the home front. When the Robinson women hear strange animal howls from beyond the force field perimeter, Maureen is adamant: "We're not going to start behaving like helpless females." When John checks in by radio to talk to Maureen—who is putting on a brave front—he senses something is amiss and returns to camp, much to the relief of the women.

Of course, the Robinson women were not constantly swooning in fear and anxiety. It was simply the man's prerogative to assume command and protect the female.

The women were expected to nurture and sustain the little colony with high spirits and good food—and so they did. The hostile dangers of an alien world barely fazed Maureen in the completion of her domestic chores (which Dr. Smith once dismissed as "dreary domestic details"). With the possible exception of an alien invasion or apocalyptic weather front, nothing kept the resourceful Mrs. Robinson from assembling everyone for meals. Maureen's spirit was unflagging. She preferred to see the proverbial glass as half-full, such as the time, with provisions running low, she gaily announced she'd "dig into the last of the flour and make us some hot biscuits."

Many an adventure revolved around Penny's own fantasy wanderings, and on an alien world there was plenty of room for a lively imagination to roam, particularly for a young lady on the way to womanhood. These fantasies had much in common with Lewis Carroll's beloved Alice, who was always finding a way to Wonderland, whether by tumbling down rabbit holes or passing through that magical looking glass. In the tale "The Magic Mirror," Penny literally did go through a mirror into a mystical dream world inhabited by a strange, lonely alien

John Robinson was always quick on the draw when some alien threat imperiled his family's space settlement.

Penny managed to live out a rich fantasy life during the Robinson's wanderings through space.

boy. In "My Friend, Mr. Nobody" Penny befriended a mysterious disembodied force who became her "imaginary friend."

A PRACTICAL MAN

But John Robinson had no time, or use, for dreaming. He had to think of daily survival, of repairing the stranded *Jupiter 2*, and of somehow completing the mission and finding a way to Alpha Centauri. The philosophy of John Robinson is summed up in the episode titled "Wish Upon a Star."

In the story, Dr. Smith has neglected his duties in the hydroponics garden, which has withered and died as a result. The long-suffering colony finally metes out punishment, banishing Smith to the wilderness (although the next morning Will brings him baked rolls with jam). While wandering off to find a new campsite, Will and Smith discover the ruins of an alien ship. In the cracked-open hull, Smith finds a magical wishing cap.

"Exactly like an Aladdin's lamp," Penny exclaims after Smith has triumphantly returned to the *Jupiter 2* camp with his prize. They discover the cap is worth two dreams a day, so they take turns conjuring up wishes. Maureen decides to "wish up something special for supper." Judy dreams up a special gown with which to dazzle Don. Penny asks for classical music tapes. And Dr. Smith is so giddy with wishes that he declares that the "thought machine" has rendered the Robot obsolete.

But Professor Robinson has other thoughts about the magic cap: "I'm a practical man and somehow I don't believe you can get something for nothing." And when Will and Penny get into an argument over the magical thinking cap, Professor Robinson lectures his daughter: "I'm very disappointed in you. You sacrificed your moral principles for something material."

Ultimately, our commander's stern warnings are proven true as the gifts decay and the alien owner reclaims the thought machine. The incident provides John Robinson a golden opportunity to impart another moral lesson to Will: "Dr. Smith asked for too much," the elder Robinson notes, "but like most people it wasn't enough. He wanted more."

"We made him leave because we were selfish," Will agrees, referring to the departed alien. At that moment a magical parting gift appears in Will's hands—a simple red apple, the perfect snack for a growing boy.

LICENSE TO KILL

But while John Robinson in outer space remained a commanding masculine presence—leader, loving husband, no-nonsense father—the pop-cultural zeitgeist back on Earth was changing. The John Wayne America of bedrock frontier values and an

unwavering moral compass was starting to slip. (In fact, in 1965 Wayne himself was recovering from his first bout with cancer, with a *Life* cover story hailing that the convalescing star was hopefully "back in action.") Certainly, director Sergio Leone's trilogy of so-called spaghetti westerns, first released in Europe in the midsixties (hitting U.S. theaters in 1967), was reshaping the western mythology. In the place of Wayne's settlers taming the frontier was Clint Eastwood's wandering bounty hunter, so rootless he didn't even have a name. All Clint's tall, bearded gunslinger knew was violence, while his morals were carved out of what sense could be made of a dusty, dangerous wasteland where desperadoes roamed like ghouls.

　　More shocking still was that English import Bond. James Bond. In *Lost in Space*'s inaugural season *Thunderball* was released, the fourth film in the

Commander John Robinson and Major West were the leaders of the Alpha Centauri mission, whether piloting through space at the controls of the Jupiter 2 *or laying down the law to some alien interloper.*

Today, after five years of peace, the world is just beginning to emerge from the searing crucible of World War III. The suffering is not yet ended. . . .
Russia is no longer a vast concentration camp of 212,000,000 victims.
Russia is free. You, the Russian people, are equal partners with all the nations of the world in the unending responsibility to keep the peace.
And this is the world's last chance.

—WALTER WINCHELL, IN "WALTER WINCHELL IN MOSCOW," COLLIER'S, OCTOBER 27, 1951

The above quote from the late newspaper columnist and broadcaster (he of the rat-a-tat-tat machine-gun delivery, famed as the narrative voice of the original *Untouchables* TV series) was a contribution to one of the strangest "what if?" scenarios ever posed by a major U.S. magazine. *Collier's* devoted its entire 1951 Halloween week issue to a fictional "Preview of the War We Do Not Want: Russia's Defeat and Occupation 1952–1960" (as the cover blurb described it). Every article in the entire magazine was written in the present tense of a future 1960, recalling an imaginary World War III and the defeat and subjugation of the Soviet Union by America-led forces of the United Nations.

The editors, in an inside editorial, touted the magazine's theme as "the most important single issue that any magazine has ever published." Certainly the cover showed they meant business: A vigilant, uniformed American wearing an "MP Occupation Forces" helmet and brandishing a rifle with a vicious-looking bayonet attached stood in front of a map of the Soviet empire pictured with United Nations flags planted in the newly "Occupied" territory. The imaginary war, which had begun in 1952 (touched off when the Soviets direct the occupation of Yugoslavia and the U.S. reacts to the "Kremlin-inspired" aggression), was conceived as ending in 1955 with the U.N. Temporary Occupation Command setting up headquarters in Moscow.

This artifact from the early years of the Cold War (although *Collier's* does not use the term in this issue) hit the newsstands during the Korean War. Korea had been a pawn in the postwar maneuvering between the U.S. and USSR, the two superpowers having occupied the south and north respectively until the country officially split in 1949. The Korean War, which broke out on June 25, 1950, when Communist North Korea invaded South Korea in a bid to unify the country, ended in July 1953 with two and a half million soldiers killed or wounded and more than three million civilian deaths.

Today's U.S. global police actions, particularly when made in conjunction with the United Nations, are hot-button political issues. But in the fifties the U.N. was seen as an instrument of U.S. policy—even God was on America's side. As *Collier's* writer Robert Sherwood put it, referring to the imaginary Third World War: "Resulting from a terrible Kremlin miscalculation [WW III] plunged a whole world into incredible horror. But the outcome was inevitable: a smashing victory for the West, and the promise of a better era." Or, as the magazine's editorial statement put it: "if the War We Do Not Want is forced upon us, we will win."

Most terrifying about the mind-set of those days is the impunity with which atomic bombs were exploded in the *Collier's* scenario. The "Red" air force drops atomic bombs on New York, Detroit, and an atomic facility in Hanford, Washington. Then, by Christmas Day on the European front, comes the report: "Atomic artillery smashes enemy offensive." But by 1953 Red A-bombers hit Chicago, New York, Washington, and Philadelphia, while nuclear subs launch strikes on five more U.S. cities, including Boston, San Francisco, and Los Angeles. Soon afterward, the U.S. unleashes another A-bomb offensive of its own at the heart of the Soviet Union, a direct hit that vaporizes twenty square miles of Moscow.

The article on the bombing mission to Moscow was famed CBS commentator Edward R. Murrow's own *Collier's* contribution, a first-person account of the fateful bomb run with pilot "Jock Mackenzie" and his crew. Murrow wrote of the moment when the bombardier announced "it's gone" as the bomb was dropped on Moscow:

As we looked down through the overcast, I saw it—something that I can only describe as the flame of a gigantic blowtorch filtering through dirty yellow gauze.

We felt nothing. It was the most professional, nerveless military operation I have ever seen. . . . I sat beside [Jock] part of the way back. At times he took over from the automatic pilot. Once he said: "It's nice to be going home. My wife and two children lived in Detroit. I haven't heard from them for over a month."

I could see his knuckles turn white as he gripped the wheel when he said it. He seemed very tired and old—anything but exultant. . . . [1]

(OPPOSITE) *A member of the U.S./U.N. Occupation Forces looms over a map of the defeated Soviet Empire. (Collier's, October 27, 1951, cover.)* (LEFT) *Political prisoners in Siberian concentration camp blast their way to freedom in this* Collier's *World War III scenario; art by William Reusswig.*

No thought was given to the ensuing nuclear winter that would have been unleashed by global nuclear exchanges, nor to the radioactive wastelands that would remain after the dust settled. Suffice to say that *Collier's*, noting the second wave of Soviet A-bomb hits on the U.S., calmly reported that domestic casualties were "greatly lessened by improved civil defense procedures."

But such was the atmosphere in post–World War II, a hangover from both the recent world war and fears of a Red world. The lurking paranoia on the home front was that instead of a fair fight the Soviets were going to infiltrate America's institutions to pervert and destroy from within, as a journalist named Edward Hunter so testified before the Congressional Committee on Un-American Activities during a March 13, 1958, hearing on "Communist Psychological Warfare."

"War has changed its form," Hunter stated. "The Communists have discovered that a man killed by a bullet is useless. He can dig no coal. . . . The objective of Communist warfare is to capture intact the minds of the people and their possessions, so they can be put to use. This is the modern conception of slavery. . . .

"The United States is the main battlefield in this Red War. I mean specifically the people and the soil and the resources of the United States."[2]

Of course, the popular culture reflected much of this angst. When the *Lost in Space* TV show debuted in 1965, saboteur Dr. Zachary Smith clearly personified America's fears of the Red Menace. Actor Jonathan Harris's character would undergo a transformation as the episodes progressed, evolving into a self-centered figure whose selfishness and sometimes outright laziness often put the Robinson camp in peril.

But in the early episodes there was no mistake—Smith was a venomous serpent. His very name—"Smith," a good old everyday American name—was the mark of the infiltrator. His title of "Doctor" seemed dangerous, emblematic of a keen mind perhaps schooled in some unspeakably twisted branch of science.

Dr. Zachary Smith was clearly a sinister force from "the other side"—the Red bogeyman come home to roost in the frontier nest of the God-fearing Robinsons.

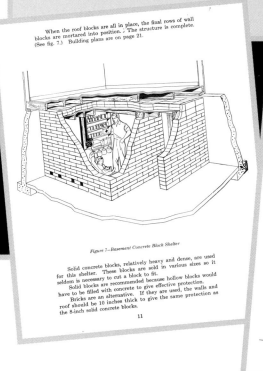

When the roof blocks are all in place, the final rows of wall blocks are mortared into position. The structure is complete. (See fig. 7.) Building plans are on page 21.

Figure 7—Basement Concrete Block Shelter

Solid concrete blocks, relatively heavy and dense, are used for this shelter. These blocks are sold in various sizes so it seldom is necessary to cut a block to fit.
Solid blocks are recommended because hollow blocks would have to be filled with concrete to give effective protection.
Bricks are an alternative. If they are used, the walls and roof should be 10 inches thick to give the same protection as the 8-inch solid concrete blocks.

11

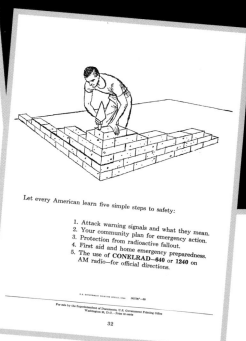

Let every American learn five simple steps to safety:

1. Attack warning signals and what they mean.
2. Your community plan for emergency action.
3. Protection from radioactive fallout.
4. First aid and home emergency preparedness.
5. The use of CONELRAD—640 or 1240 on AM radio—for official directions.

U.S. GOVERNMENT PRINTING OFFICE: 1960   O—552758

For sale by the Superintendent of Documents, U.S. Government Printing Office
Washington 25, D.C. - Price 15 cents

32

During the Cold War it was a given that concrete and brick would defend home and family from radioactive fallout. (The Family Fallout Shelter, U.S. Government publication, 1960.)

Dr. Smith never saw an alien menace he couldn't shriek at and run away from—unless, of course, Will was handy to use as a human shield.

adventures of 007, the spy who was "licensed to kill." As *The Psychotronic Encyclopedia of Film* puts it: "The fourth Bond movie really ushered in the '60s spy mania. Soon we had films with Matt Helm, Derek Flint, Harry Palmer, and endless European imitations and spoofs. *Get Smart*, *I Spy*, and *The Girl from U.N.C.L.E.* joined *The Man from U.N.C.L.E.* on television. Plastic suitcases with hidden daggers and revolvers were must-have items for the hip elementary school student. *Playboy* showed us the Bond girls in scenes that were never in the movies."[3]

Actor Sean Connery gave the early Bond age a suave style. But beneath the character's cool exterior was a cold-blooded assassin, an agent who could quip as he killed. And when each mission's Mr. Big was finally encountered it was the chance to kick up the adrenaline level, to get serious about the game of death without the mess of wasting the cheap lives of lower-level subordinates.

Author Ian Fleming's Bond novels were produced during the first fearsome decade of the Cold War. A war without shooting called for a new kind of hero, one who got by on an assassin's stealth—hail the superspy. The clean, cool kills were usually one-on-one affairs, forays celebrated in Top Secret documents or on a need-to-know basis.

Bond was a cynical, world-weary loner for whom women were merely pleasurable distractions (Bond tried marriage once—it didn't work out).

There were certainly no children of his own to teach, no little domestic nest to protect. It was an ideology, not home and family, that Bond was hired to protect. The only morality for the superspy was that given him by the state.

The Bond movies, with their villains threatening world domination with awesome weapons of destruction, were certainly not far from the deadly reality of foreign foes with fingers on nuclear triggers. Audiences could relate to the fantastic gadgets in Bond's personal arsenal—they seemed like the real-world spin-offs of Space Age technology.

And whether high-tech gadgets or apocalyptic reports of atmospheric ozone thinning, global climate change, nuclear plant disasters scorching entire regions, or rumors of atomic bombs falling into the wrong hands, it became more apparent, closer down the timeline to 1997, that we were all living in a Bond world.

"As the twentieth century spins out of control world problems and crises take on bizarre, Bondian hues," *Spy* magazine observed in a 1988 article.

". . . Let us play among the stars . . ." John (with his flying pack strapped on) and Maureen—America's first couple in space!

"Civilian airlines get shot out of the sky, space shuttles explode—it's the stuff of every Bond movie's overproduced precredit sequence. Crop failures, first in the Soviet Union and then in the American Midwest, seem less explicable as random global catastrophes than as the results of machinations by pan-European super villains. What is the Greenhouse Effect if not the grand design of a [Bond villains] Blofeld or a Drax?"[4]

There would be darker, more amoral heroes in the decades to come, from gun-toting urban vigilantes in the movies to brooding comic book superheroes who had the nasty mean streaks that used to be an exclusive characteristic of villains.

But since *Lost in Space* never had an official ending, a final episode in which to conclude the storyline—in those days most canceled shows simply went off the air—the mission still goes on, unto the end of syndication. John Robinson is truly lost in space, eternally vigilant, with jaw forward, teeth gritted, eyes squinting into alien suns. A patrician presence for all time.

MARTA KRISTEN

Marta Kristen's character of Judy Robinson seemed to have it all: a beautiful young woman who, with her loving TV family, could face the deadliest threat unafraid. Real life was more complicated. Marta Kristen was born toward the end of World War II to an unwed Finnish mother who, when Marta's German soldier father died on the Russian front, put two-month-old Marta up for adoption. Thankfully, at the age of five, she was adopted by a loving couple in Michigan who raised her as their own, even allowing her the freedom to move to California to pursue a career in Hollywood (which included being in the run for the title role in Stanley Kubrick's *Lolita*).

In a strange twist of fate, the celebrity of her role on *Lost in Space* led to a reunion with her biological mother and blood brothers and sisters. While this *Lost* connection to her mother occurred in 1969, lightning struck again in 1997 as more *Lost in Space* publicity helped bridge the gap with a brother she never knew she had.

Professionally, Kristen's work has ranged from episodic television and commercial spots to work in theater. One of her favorite roles was in *Wings*, a 1995 play in which she played a death-defying, high-flying wing walker who suffers a stroke. "I like stories of strength and courage in the face of adversity," she says of her *Wings* role—a heartfelt connection mirrored in her own life experience.

Two months after I was born on February 26, 1945, I was put in an orphanage in Norway. My mother had signed the papers to put me up for adoption, but no one would adopt me because of my half-German-half-Finnish heritage. In the orphanage the other kids called me "that Nazi child," which was very difficult. There was one little girl named Eva, who was sort of my surrogate mother and she would comfort me. A social worker named Marta Bentzen was like an aunt to me—I got my first name from her—and I corresponded with tanta [aunt] Marta until she died in the seventies.

I was finally adopted at age five and went to Michigan to live with Harold and Bertha Soderquist. Astounding people; I was so incredibly lucky to have been adopted by them. In the early eighties they were the oldest members of the Peace Corps. They are both recently deceased, but each lived to be ninety-eight years old.

*When **Lost in Space** was canceled I was married and in about the fourth month of my pregnancy. I didn't think about it then, but it was ironic that in **Lost in Space** I was part of this family that was so loving, caring, and cohesive while off-screen I was having terrible troubles with my marriage. I think one of the reasons I married very young was I was just looking for a family.*

*Soon after the show was canceled I received a telegram from the studio [Twentieth Century Fox] saying somebody was telegraphing from Finland saying she was my mother. This came about because I had done a **Lost in Space** interview with a Finnish fan magazine called **Aida** in which I'd mentioned my mother had been Finnish and her name was Helmi Rusanen. My older sister, Anneli Rusanen, happened to read this article in a coffee shop in Helsinki—and she never reads fan magazines! She later told me she felt as if her heart was going to leap from her chest because she'd remembered a photograph of our mother with an infant girl that wasn't her, but nothing had ever been said about it. She went to Helmi who broke down and said that yes, I was her daughter and she'd never told anybody about me. So Anneli instigated contact with me. I telephoned Anneli, who speaks beautiful English, and we decided I should visit them in Finland. So in the summer of 1969 I took my adopted parents to see my Finnish family. My husband, who wasn't supportive, didn't go on the trip.*

Seeing my real mother was very, very difficult. Helmi and my adopted mother actually got along very well. They communicated through my sister and father, who spoke Swedish fluently. But I was frozen. Every night I had nightmares of running, fears of being trapped, of losing the child that I was carrying. I hadn't expected those emotions.

Then we took a ferry to Sweden and across to Norway to the orphanage so I could see Marta again. It felt like a completion to go back and see the many people who had helped me. It was a saga, a review of my life up to that point.

Then I traveled by myself through Europe for two months as I got bigger and bigger with my pregnancy. I heard from my husband twice and that was about it. I traveled by train everywhere. I was in Capri when the first moon landing happened. When I came home I had my daughter Laura. Three years later I left my husband. In 1974, I met my husband-to-be, Kevin, and we've been together ever since.

In March of 1997 I was in Australia with June Lockhart doing a **Lost in Space** interview for Australian television hosted by a popular personality named Peter Luck. On this show I mentioned I had a family in Finland and about the circumstances of meeting them through **Lost in Space**. Well, later that summer my sister Anneli got a call from a woman named Paivi Rusanen who said she thought her husband Seppo was our brother! The funny thing with Seppo was that he and his wife rarely watch television, but Paivi was channel surfing and saw this **Lost in Space** interview.

The records bear out that Seppo, when he was six months old, was taken in by a Finnish couple who, curiously enough, never adopted him. This couple had told Seppo about Helmi, and even that I might be his sister, but they didn't want him to pursue it. They had recently passed away and on his fiftieth birthday he thought it was finally time to find out if indeed this Rusanen family in Finland and America was his.

When my sister told me we had a brother in Australia, she also let the other shoe drop and mentioned we had **another** sister, Leena, in Finland. We figured we probably shared the same father with Leena, while Helmi had Seppo two years afterward with a different father. My mother was very fertile, to say the least.

Marta (LEFT) *on 1997* Lost in Space *movie set, ready for her cameo role.*

I received a letter from Seppo the very day of the **Lost in Space** launch on October 16, 1997. I was actually reading the letter on my way to an event honoring the launch at the Museum of Television and Radio in Beverly Hills. His letter was so beautifully written, about all the years he'd known this information but hadn't wanted to pursue it. He wrote of finding his soul mate, having children, and their life in a beautiful area outside of Sydney. But the letter was also full of trepidation and pain about abandonment and whether he really should be pursuing his past. I think he was afraid of being rejected and hurt. He wrote, "I'll understand if you don't answer this, but I hope that you do." I wrote back saying that yes, I believed he was my brother.

In 1989, my husband and our daughter, Laura, went back to Finland without my adopted parents and had a wonderful time. Helmi was still alive but by then she was starting to show the first signs of Alzheimer's disease. She never once complained, by the way, about anything. Very strong lady. During that visit I told Helmi I wasn't angry with her. In fact, she had done me the best possible favor. I'd ended up with this wonderful, interesting life. We both broke down and cried.

On this trip I'd wanted to find out about my real father and his family but all Helmi could remember was his name was Hans. But the Germans and Finns kept records from the war. I'm sure I can find him in the records. That's my next project.

The Robinson space shuttle runs into some big trouble. Decades later Bill Mumy would pen a song about how Will Robinson "shot the one-eyed giant down with laser in my hand."

⑤ DANGER, WILL ROBINSON!

In American fiction there's a tradition of enterprising boys who wade with abandon into the adult world. In literature there's the exploits of Huck and Tom, and the treasure-hunting adventures of Jim Hawkins. Tom Swift (both senior and junior) was always tinkering with some fantastic new invention, while the Hardy Boys never turned their backs on a mystery. In the comic book world of costumed superheroes, a youthful sidekick was de rigueur ever since Batman answered the Batsignal's call with Robin at his side. Movies, particularly in the golden age of the studio system, loved kids in a group dynamic, whether the zany innocence of the Little Rascals or the streetwise shenanigans of the Dead End Kids.

A BOY AND HIS FATHER

Will Robinson was no exception from this tradition, but his independence was tempered by his love of duty and alliance to father and family. Will was always eager to help his dad and Major West fortify and defend the camp, engage in a reconnaissance mission, or do the usual sweat work you'd encounter on another world (whether hunting for ore samples or building a water-purifying system). Will embodied the venerable Boy Scout slogans: "A scout is trustworthy, loyal, helpful, friendly, courteous, kind; a scout is obedient, cheerful, thrifty, brave, clean, reverent." Once, when Dr. Smith told Will he was "the most talented of all the Robinsons," the boy just shrugged off the flattery with the comment: "I try to do my job."

Of course, many a *Lost* tale revolved around the lad's eagerness to impress his dad by tackling some dangerous task. And, of course, in his attempts to please and achieve, Will sometimes suffered his father's reprimands. "From now on, before you leap into anything, I want you to stop, think, *and consult me*," his father once sternly told him. Another lecture began, "Will, you happen to be a very bright, a very talented boy," then the kicker: "but you're still a boy." Will always sheepishly took those lectures

A boy's Christmas dreams drift to thoughts of the fantastic future of space in this Astounding *cover painting by H. R. Van Dongen.*

without complaint, nodding with eyes downcast and a muttered "Yes, sir." This was no wisecracking kid: His father's approval was enough to have Will floating on a cloud of joy, and he always respectfully called his old man "Sir."

This was, after all, the alternate TV dimensional year of 1997, where institutions and authority figures still commanded respect. And as a fictional figure Will was expected to be a good role model for a youthful, impressionable audience. A boy like Will didn't talk back to his father or disrespect his mother. It simply wasn't done. "Everybody *did* sit down to dinner together back then," *Lost* concept artist Roy Alexander recalls, "and back then the family unit was regularly portrayed on television."

Mark Moore, creative director of the ILM art department, was about Will's age when he watched the original TV show. During the season when the flashy new *Batman* series was competing in the same time slot with *Lost in Space,* there was even a brief tussle for his affections, with the Robinson family saga ultimately winning out. Moore recalls the positive message of one particular episode:

"I remember one show ["Follow the Leader"] where there was an alien presence controlling John Robinson through this helmet he was wearing. He took his son to the edge of this cliff, and was going to throw Will over the edge when his son goes, 'Can I talk to my dad one more time?' John Robinson takes off the helmet. 'Dad, I just want to tell you that I love you.' And then his dad, who's been in the control of this alien, regains his humanity and throws the helmet over. The episode ended with the moral that love is the ultimate power in the universe. Wow! I always thought that was pretty good for a weekly television show."

BOY STUFF

Like all boys, curiosity drove Will into many an adventure. After discovering an abandoned "robotoid," Will, with his father's permission, activated the mechanical creation—much to the consternation of their own loyal Robot. Complications ensued.

Once, when a "matter transfer unit" left behind by an alien species was discovered, the mysterious technological device was put "off limits" to our curious Will. "This gizmo is irresistible to a boy like Will," Don warned John. And, of course, Will *couldn't* resist a device that could instantly transport him through space, particularly when he believed he might be able to get back to Earth and alert Alpha Control about the plight of his family. (Will's voyage to Earth and back is chronicled in the episode "Return from Outer Space.")

To Will, girls were clearly strange, inscrutable characters. Being of good heart, Will once presented Penny with a necklace of diamonds she'd discovered in her own wanderings. "You know how girls are," he shrugged later, "always liking useless stuff."

In many ways, Will is the heart of *Lost in Space,* a fearless scrapper full of the bravery and innocence of youth. As the TV program itself evolved over the course of its three-season run, Will took center stage. "Irwin Allen wanted the series to become 'Treasure Island in Space,'" notes Foxstar producer Kevin Burns. "It became a story about a boy and his robot, with Dr. Smith as Long John Silver."

"ADMIRABLY STRAIGHT"

One of Will's shining moments was the first-season episode "Invaders from the Fifth Dimension." The Robinsons' first settlement on a deserted world was

Father and son confer—across the decades. Lost in Space movie incarnation features Jack Johnson as Will and William Hurt as John Robinson.

THE WHIZ KID

Boys—join the young inventor Tom Swift Jr. in strange and exciting new adventures you won't want to miss. . . .
Tom is the son of a famous inventor who, in his time, created so many of the wonders of today long before they were actually built . . . submarine, television, giant tanks, and many others. Now, Tom and his friend, Bud Barclay, invent, build and test dozens of powerful atomic devices.

—BACK COVER COPY FOR TOM SWIFT AND HIS FLYING LAB, 1954,
THE FIRST IN THE SERIES OF TOM SWIFT JR. ADVENTURES

Tom Senior, the fictional young inventor who through some thirty-eight novels released between 1910 and 1941 invented wonders for the Machine Age (such as his 1933 "television detector"), provided the sage presence as his eighteen-year-old son got the *Swift* franchise going again in the mid-fifties. Junior was ready and eager to dream up a new generation of Space Age inventions for that transitional era when science fantasy was rapidly changing into science fact.

Will Robinson, ever curious, resourceful, and inventive, would have loved hooking up with Tom Jr. It was at Swift Enterprises that Tom created everything from a jetmarine (a two-man submarine to help overcome pirate scientists in that adventure) to an atomic earth blaster (to penetrate the South Pole in pursuit of mineral resources).

But young Swift's greatest achievement was in single-handedly leading the way into outer space. In his first adventure, our young hero got his atomic-powered, winged Sky Queen Flying Lab off the ground: "This plane is just one step this side of a trip to the planets," his sidekick Bud told Tom. Swift Jr. also battled a sinister Eurasian (!) mercenary, discovered a new atomic ore (dubbed "Swiftonium"), and took possession of a contact probe sent to Earth from an alien civilization.

Each Swift story promised "new inventions in the world of tomorrow." In the 1955 adventure *Tom Swift and*

once again visited by strange aliens. Within the darkness of the visiting space ship floated their disembodied heads, representing the fifth-dimensional space in which they dwelled. These aliens, feeling their mental powers waning, had come in search of a human brain they could tap into (strangely so, since one of the aliens dissed Earth as "a minor planetoid in a near-barbaric state of development"). The aliens considered Dr. Smith's brain but passed, telling him

that his inherent treachery and cunning indicated "defective relays in your reasoning circuits." But Will Robinson's lively young brain matter seemed the perfect cerebral rejuvenator. "Your moral programming is admirably straight," the aliens told Will.

As the aliens prepared to take him away to their world, they ordered Will to clear his mind so they could erase his mental circuits. Tears streaked down the freckled cheeks of the brave little boy. He

His Outpost in Space, the boy wonder and company got a space station into orbit. (This breakthrough was consistent with the early fifties reality that envisioned orbiting space platforms for military purposes and as a pit stop on the way to the moon and planets beyond.) The gigantic hub-and-spoke-shaped outpost was done up with labs, a cosmic observatory, polished mirrors to catch the sun's rays for a solar-battery system, and a radio and TV station that could relay programs over a third of the planet (anticipating the television communications satellites to come).

By the 1958 adventure *Tom Swift in the Race to the Moon*, the boy inventor had made friends with beings from another planet. In his moon-bound rocketship *Challenger* (also the future name of the space shuttle that in January 1986 tragically exploded soon after liftoff), Swift also beat out "foreign enemies" to make the first manned moon landing.

Swift and his crew's first lunar sight was of "jagged mountain ranges, yawning cracks and craters, great darkened plains." As *Challenger* set down in the Crater of Copernicus, the crew let out a cheer, with Bud exclaiming: "Tom Swift, first earthman to reach the Moon! . . . You're a wonder, pal!"

Of course, our all-American, modest young hero wasn't about to hog all the glory. He smiled, said thanks, then grew serious: "I just want to say that everyone here has helped me to reach our destination."

Such were the virtues of America's surrogate teen-in-space. Fearless and willing to brave the frontier of space, but happy to return to Mother Earth.

There was the time that Tom, after spending thirty days aboard his orbiting space shuttle, returned to Earth in pure "aw, shucks" mode. He was greeted by newsreel and television camera crews, while police battled "to keep back the cheering, flag-waving crowds who turned out to do honor to the inventor of the first outpost in space."

Tom greeted the media with a smile, glanced skyward, then noted: "Next visit up there, I'm going to head for a satellite of Mars. But right now—you can quote me on this—it's good to be back on the planet Earth!"

couldn't get his family out of his mind. The aliens' mind-probing computer began to short-circuit.

"Love—what is it?" one of the floating alien heads exclaimed, ordering Will to stop such nonsense. "Can you eat it? What does it do? What primitive, barbaric little creatures you are! On your own planet you slaughter each other unceasingly—all in the name of love."

"At least we keep trying to get better," Will snapped back. "We don't go around turning people into machines."

The aliens realized it was useless to go on. They couldn't break Will's "mental circuits of emotional blockages." Will was magically transported back outside the alien ship, and he embraced his mother and father just as the ship exploded.

Don't mess with Robinson family unity—it's stronger than any alien mind-probing computer.

SCIENCE FUN AND FACT

"It . . . it's getting warmer! I'm . . . I'm entering the atmosphere!"
The heat increased! The plasto space suit began to sizzle . . .
its outer limits burning away . . .
Epilogue: When a falling object from outer space enters the Earth's atmosphere,
it begins to BURN from the friction caused by its passing through the air
at such great speed!

—A SPACE "ROCKET-PILOT" FLOATS FROM THE WRECK OF HIS ROCKETSHIP INTO THE PLANET'S
ATMOSPHERE—WITH RESULTS EXPLAINED IN THE TALE "HOME TO STAY!" FROM E.C. CLASSIC REPRINT
NO. 5, WEIRD FANTASY #13, 1973

The above space disaster, originally published by E.C. comics in 1952, has a boy of the future watching the night sky and making a wish for his space dad's safe return as he catches sight of a falling star—unaware that the shooting streak is his own father burning up in the atmosphere.

Such heart-warming tales stirred the outrage of the nation's adults, leading to the end of comic books like *The Vault of Horror* and *Tales from the Crypt*, but one can't fault the E.C. editors for making sure young readers understood the principle of atmospheric vaporization!

Science fiction has always been a vehicle for both flights of fantasy and the posing of possible science scenarios, often with some science fact thrown in for good measure. And back with the launch of *Sputnik*—and the United States' renewed commitment to teaching young people basic science in order to compete in an overheated Cold War atmosphere—even comic books began to increasingly mix fact with fun.

Case in point: DC Comics' sixties incarnation of its classic forties superhero the Flash—the fastest man alive!—often incorporated tidbits of science fact in the fantastic tales. In one 1965 story the Flash tried to see how fast he could run, his thought balloons noting the measuring devices he wore to record his effort to "hit Roemer-10"—more than 1,860,000 miles a second, or around the world 75 times in a single second! A helpful editor's note added: "Just as Mach−1 is used to denote the speed of sound in honor of the Austrian physicist Ernst Mach—so Flash credits Danish astronomer Olaus Roemer—discoverer of the velocity of light . . . "[1] (Flash did hit his Roemer-10 mark, but soon discovered the feat had an unintended consequence—it gave him mental telepathy!)

A natural for a commingling of science fiction and fact was the adventures of Adam Strange, a Buck Rogers clone (Buck had his Wilma, Adam his Alanna) and star of the DC Comics title *Mystery in Space*. Interspersed throughout each issue would be such one-page illustrated true-science features as "Giants of the Telescope," "Amazing Asteroids," or "Our Amazing Universe!"

Nuggets of science fact were also leavened in within the action of the Adam Strange stories themselves. No cosmic conflict was too threatening, no situation too dire, to keep Strange from commenting on the intricacies of natural phenomena.

Once, while flying through the north pole of an alien world, Strange started rhapsodizing to his beloved Alanna about Earth's own aurora borealis, which is "caused by streams of electrically charged particles emitted by the sun striking the upper atmosphere." In another adventure, Strange, contemplating ways to defeat a superpowered alien, observed a thundercloud and was off on a description of a storm cloud's capacity for producing lightning when "positively charged drops cluster at the top of the cloud, the negatively charged ones at the bottom."

Then there was the time that leaders of every nation on the planet Rann looked to Strange for the answer to defeating flying flame-covered "sun-beings" wreaking havoc on their world. In a demonstration before the assembled leaders, Strange mixed a can of baking soda and a bottle of vinegar in an empty glass, producing carbon dioxide gas. "On Earth we use this colorless, odorless gas to put out fires," Strange noted, using the demo mixture to extinguish a candle flame.

Thus armed with barrels of carbon dioxide gas—and while riding on the backs of gigantic fireflies—Strange led an attack that literally extinguished the sun-beings. A world saved—because someone knew his science!

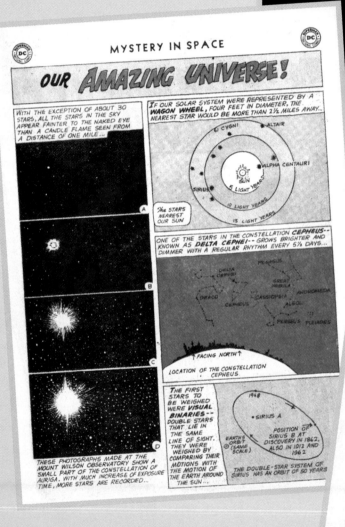

(LEFT) *In the pop cultural landscape of the sixties, it was permissible—even encouraged—to mix fact with fun, such as this regular "Our Amazing Universe!" feature in the DC Comics title* Mystery in Space. *(Note, in the top right panel, the location of the Robinsons' own mission destination of Alpha Centauri.)* (BELOW) *In another fun/fact fusion, space traveler Adam Strange and his girlfriend Alanna compare the natural phenomena of planet Rann with Earth.* (Mystery in Space, *Issue #75, May 1962, DC Comics.)*

BILL MUMY

Bill Mumy, who will forever be engraved in pop cultural consciousness as the plucky, heroic young Will Robinson, is fond of noting that "show business does not eat its young," particularly when one is doing what they love to do.

Mumy *is* loving it, and proving there's life after *Lost in Space*, amassing numerous movie and television credits (including an estimated 400-plus television episodes), co-creating the program *Space Cases* for Nickelodeon, being a series cast member on *Babylon 5* since 1993, and currently developing a science fiction project with his friend and colleague Mark Hamill (Will Robinson meet Luke Skywalker!).

Mumy, the son of a wealthy cattle rancher, grew up in Los Angeles and fondly recalls carefree days taking the bus to the beach and staying out until dark, the fun of searching out Hollywood magic shops, and other innocent pleasures. "I think things were better then across the board," he says with a backward glance.

Mumy remembers his Will Robinson days as a formative time not only because of his youth but because he had become one of the lead stars of *Lost in Space*. "The series had certainly shifted from the theme of the pilot—the adventures of a pioneering family alone against the alien elements—to a fantasy-comedy that focused on Jonathan, the Robot, and myself. Certainly Guy [Williams] had a diminished role considering what he'd expected. But I cherish the scenes we had together. He taught me to fence. He was always pleasant. I miss him."

Williams, who passed away in 1989, inspired a very young Mumy to enter into that phantasmagoric landscape on the other side of television's looking-glass screen. Williams, who played the role of the black-masked, swashbuckling Zorro of TV fame, was one of those heroes of the tube who entranced a young kid brimming with energy and imagination.

Guy Williams actually inspired me to become an actor because I was a huge Zorro *fan. When I was four years old I actually broke my leg playing Zorro. I had jumped off my bed, which I imagined was a fort wall, onto a Bozo Bop clown I was convinced was the evil comandante and landed on a metal Winchester toy rifle and cracked my leg bone in half. I spent almost twelve weeks in a cast staring at the TV set watching Guy Williams as Zorro and George Reeves as Superman. I wanted to be an adventurer on TV. I begged my parents to make that happen and they were very supportive.*

I loved being Will Robinson; he was a dream come true. Here was Will, a boy astronaut and adventurer, dressed in his little superhero outfit with a laser gun in his hand shooting a giant cyclops, fixing all the things no one else could fix, saving the day week after week. What wasn't to like? The thing with playing Will was that I played it straight through the whole series. You knew Will believed it, which is why I think so many people related to him.

We made Lost in Space *during a brief period of pop art consciousness. But I can't compare the television of then to now because they're almost like different mediums. No one thought that the TV show you were making in 1965 would, thirty years later, be running daily all over the planet. When we made* Lost in Space*, television had only been dominant in people's lives for little more than a decade. Back then you didn't have sixty-four channels, cable, VCRs, and videotape. It was a whole different cultural reality. But I think the moral values and quality of entertainment we got in the sixties was a lot better than the stuff we're producing today. My wife and I have two children [Seth, age 8, and Liliana, age 3]. I'm sorry they're not exposed to programming with more positive messages. Things I watched as a kid, like the classic episodes of* Superman*, taught me to be a good guy. Now within the comic book superhero genre alone there's been at least ten years of this awful antihero thing.*

I've had a great run so far. I've worked with all these great people: Alfred Hitchcock, Walt Disney, Lucille Ball, Rod Serling, Jimmy Stewart. I did three episodes of **Twilight Zone** and Rod Serling was warm and funny; he wasn't an imposing presence when he walked on a set, like Irwin Allen was. I made a movie called **Dear Brigitte** with Jimmy Stewart and he was the best of the best, the greatest gentleman.

Hitchcock was a sadistic bastard. I did three episodes of **Alfred Hitchcock Presents**, including one he directed called "Bang, You're Dead." Actually, Marta Kristen had a small part in that episode as well. That was 1961 and it was a six-day shoot. I was in almost every shot. Toward the end of the shoot, near the end of a long day, they needed to get a close-up done before I could leave. I was squirming around on my mark; I couldn't keep still. Then, from behind the camera, Hitchcock comes waddling up to me. He was this imposing figure who always wore these ridiculously tight white shirts with his jowls hanging over the collar, black suits, and black ties. He was constantly sweating. He leans down to my ear so only I can hear and said—and this is **exactly** what he said—"If you don't stop moving about, I'm going to get a nail and I'm going to nail your feet to your mark and blood will come pouring out like milk. So stop moving." I was totally petrified and stood still like a statue. Then they shot their close-up.

Afterward, I told my mother about it and she said, "Oh, honey, he's British, they have a different sense of humor." The point is all he had to do after he got the shot was to call me over and tell me he'd just been teasing. But he **loved** the fact that he petrified me. From that day on I never wanted to see him again. Hitchcock had an office right on the main drive at Universal and whenever I had to go on the lot I'd go out of my way to avoid his office, taking a detour around a couple of soundstages, because I didn't want to bump into him.

But most of the people I've worked with have been pretty nice. The entertainment business is the most collaborative in the world, and most of the people in it understand that. You need a good team to make something work.

THE BALLAD OF WILLIAM ROBINSON

My name is William Robinson, I'm forty-two years old;
I've seen the hot side of the sun, I've seen blue icy cold;
I've shot the one-eyed giant down with laser in my hand,
    but I'll never see my home again or walk on Earth's green land;
In 1997 we set out on the **Jupiter 2** bound for Alpha Centauri,
    my family and small crew, we ran into a meteor storm the
    wrong time, the wrong place;
It's been six months and thirty years that we've been lost in space;
My father died five years ago, there was no better man than he,
    my mother's never been the same, and now it's up to me;
Our pilot is a handsome man, my sisters both could tell;
And Doctor Smith will get us killed and that may be just as well;
I've worked the mines of many worlds for fuel to power our ship;
I've got a Robot for a friend and helper on our trip;
I'm sending out this message now from this ungodly place
    in hopes someone will rescue us from being lost in space;
My name is William Robinson and I'll never take a wife,
    no children will I father, I have no normal life;
Show me mercy in this universe or show me God's true face;
Whisper my name to the stars, for I am lost in space.

   —Lyrics by Bill Mumy from his album **Dying** to Be Heard,
      Renaissance Records, copyright 1997

(OPPOSITE) *The* Lost *cast gathers round to celebrate Bill Mumy's birthday.*
(ABOVE) *Bill Mumy.*
(Photo by Bobby Klein)

Penny gets in step with a visiting alien.

6 WELCOME TO THE FUN COLONY

You'll get all the action you want after you've persuaded Will to drop his hang-ups and make our scene—not his folks'!

—BARTHOLOMEW, THE ALIEN TEENAGER WHO CAN NEVER GROW UP, TALKING TO DR. SMITH, FROM "THE PROMISED PLANET," LOST IN SPACE EPISODE SEVENTY-EIGHT, SEASON THREE

It's like freaky, man, real freaky!

—DR. SMITH AS A SPACE HIPPIE, FROM "THE PROMISED PLANET," LOST IN SPACE EPISODE SEVENTY-EIGHT, SEASON THREE

In the third season of *Lost in Space*, our fearless space-traveling family unfortunately became lost in that most hallucinatory of all places: the fevered dimension of sixties pop/camp culture.

SPACE CAMP

Perhaps it was the giddy thrill of having transitioned from the monochromatic palette of that first all black-and-white season to bright color schemes that made it easy to stray into pop/camp territory. The dawn of an all-color age was celebrated in the second season's first episode, with the *Jupiter 2* barely escaping the explosion of the planet upon which they had been stranded most of the first season.

Perhaps it was the campy influence of the *Batman* TV show, still at its height of popularity, that caused the *Lost* plots to drift from the character-driven, family values stories of the first two seasons. "You bet I watched *Lost in Space*, although I got very impatient with it after the second season," says ILM's Ned Gorman. "The first season in particular it was semiserious. Dr. Smith was a real villain,

and you really felt for the plight of these people marooned on the other side of the galaxy. But then it started getting very surreal and campy. I don't know whether it was because Irwin Allen was doing that to keep it fresh or responding to what people wanted. After all, it was the sixties and people as a collective consciousness got screwier. Perhaps he was responding to that.

"Unlike film, where it'll take years to get something through development, in TV, for better or worse, you have to keep your finger on the pulse of the public throughout a season," Gorman continues. "I'm sure that half the people working in television back then were weekend hippies experimenting with drugs. And one could safely assume there was a fair amount of people laying that in between the lines of their scripts. Now whether that got past a producer, who knows?"

Most veterans of Irwin Allen's TV productions agree that his shows were launched with strong production values and dramatic situations, but no one has a final answer for exactly why Allen's TV productions would eventually drift into camp territory. Like an early experimental rocket shot, the trajectory of an Allen-produced series would crest and then crash smack into the Pop landscape of pure camp.

"We didn't do it to Paul's face, but we used to kid Paul Zastupnevich, the costume designer, about the 'vegetable of the week,'" Roy Alexander recalls, "some of the ridiculous, threatening characters that would be discovered on each planet as they bogeyed through space each week. It seems all of Irwin's shows took on that aspect after a while. At one time on both *Lost in Space* and *Voyage to the Bottom of the Sea* it was like the monster of the week. I don't know whether it was the appetite of the audience at the time or Irwin's true bent coming to the surface."

The *Lost in Space* cast and fans always single out "The Great Vegetable Rebellion," the second-to-last episode of the entire series, as one of the camp classics. It's high-concept: The Robinsons visit a strange planet and encounter Tybo, a giant carrot who attempts to turn them all into vegetables, getting as far as transforming Smith into a living stalk of celery. Cast members to this day cheerily admit it was a struggle to keep a straight face while reciting melodramatic dialogue to a guy in a big carrot suit.

SPACE FREAKING

But the episode that was probably the biggest camp riff on that turned-on era was "The Promised Planet," another of the final episodes in the show's three-year run. Broadcast on January 24, 1968, the show was a *Lost* take on the hippie phenomenon. The previous summer had seen the unfolding of the famed "Summer of Love" in San Francisco, the apex of the hippie movement. Those years were a bright flash of turned-on youth, acid rock festivals, and rebellion in all its forms, from long-hair fashions to campus political demonstrations.

In the "Promised Planet" episode, the *Jupiter 2* crew, convinced that they've found the gateway to their mission goal of Alpha Centauri, land on the planet Delta. A colony there is run by human-looking teenagers who are really aliens in disguise, beings unable to grow into maturity—and they don't dig it at all. "All I want to be able to do is *shave*, see," cried one of the poor Peter Pan-ish aliens at the end.

What camp wonders are in this episode? Consider: A psychedelic "display of electronics pyrotechnics" as the *Jupiter 2* descends into the planet's atmosphere ("Enjoy, enjoy," the Robot exclaims); a light show that drives Penny into a go-go dancing frenzy ("Fight—you've got to resist it," an impassioned Will shouts as Penny grooves); a battle of wills as the aliens try to convince Will and Penny not to play the "olders game"; plenty of cool battle-of-the-generations stuff as the aliens try to persuade Will and Penny to go to Planet Gamma ("it's a fun colony"); and then there's Penny, hypnotized by those darn teen aliens, *talking back to her dad*: "Here it comes, that sentimental gunk about parents and their children . . . olders are out—we're in." Most wonderful of all is the vision of Zach Smith transformed into a moptopped space hippie who inexplicably hangs out playing pool, striking the pose of a hustler from a fifties biker flick while flanked by two spaced-out painted hippie chicks. ("You can't turn on at your age, Dr. Smith," Penny huffs, delivering the ultimate put-down.)

When John Robinson and company's memory was momentarily taken away—and they briefly left Will, Penny, and Smith behind on planet Delta—all was set to rights when they inhaled some suspicious "memory cones." "Light 'em up and find out," Robot suggested to a momentarily memory-drained John Robinson, who was wondering what to do with the cones.

"We're going to freak out together. I'm way out, man," was the rap hippie Smith laid down before a sober John Robinson returned to rescue them all.

(ABOVE) *After its first black-and-white season, Lost in Space drifted ever deeper into the currents of the camp aesthetic of the mid- to late sixties (as witnessed in this gaudy scene of a space babe taking her ease).*
(LEFT) *Dr. Smith recoils from Tybo, the carrot ruler of a vegetable world—or is Smith merely reacting to the delicious awfulness of "The Great Vegetable Rebellion," the next-to-last episode in the series? "TV Guide listed it as one of the one hundred top episodes of all time," Bill Mumy says, wincing. "I think it's a great example of one of the worst television shows ever conceived, much less shot. It's like an Ed Wood movie. Guy and June laughed so much through the whole thing they were written out of the next episode."*

(RIGHT) *A mop-topped Smith gets down and freaky in "The Promised Planet."*
(BELOW) *As usual, Smith is betrayed by aliens as the young humans populating planet Delta are revealed to be of more exotic, alien stock.*

LIVE FROM THE MOON

I believe this nation should commit itself to achieving the goal, before this decade is out, of landing a man on the Moon and returning him safely to Earth.

—PRESIDENT JOHN F. KENNEDY, ADDRESS TO CONGRESS, MAY 25, 1961

If the astronauts have landed on the Moon, the networks will stay with the mission throughout the night, preempting regular programming. . . .
If the mission proceeded on schedule, the astronauts will begin their walk on the Moon at about 11:15 P.M. A black-and-white TV camera will be set up on the lunar surface.

—TV GUIDE *SUNDAY PROGRAMMING NOTICES FOR JULY 20, 1969,*
ISSUE FOR THE WEEK OF JULY 19 TO 25

In the December 17, 1965, issue of *Life* there appeared a six-page foldout prepared by artist Robert Rauschenberg titled "A Modern Inferno," ostensibly honoring the 700th birthday of the poet Dante. Billed as a "modern interpretation" of the poet's immortal poem the *Inferno* (which described Dante and Virgil's descent through the many rings of hell), Rauschenberg's work featured a silk-screened montage of photographic images. The journey into the modern inferno began with a "careening motorcyclist" headed into a hellish panorama: shots of Hitler's henchmen and World War II death camps, glimpses of the hooded Klan, atomic mushroom clouds, images of bomb-blasted cities and auto wreckage . . .

"And in the midst appear two astronauts," read the accompanying text. "Like Dante and Virgil they are voyagers into unearthly realms. . . . These travelers stand apart from the earth like detached witnesses, observing the accelerating force of dehumanizing machines and the bestiality that threatens to destroy man."[1]

In 1965 Americans were experiencing both the agony and the ecstasy of space travel. Some Americans saw the astronauts as mythic figures, with space travel a race for salvation. But there were legions of critics demanding why so much money—nearly $30 billion by 1969—was being spent on Buck Rogers dreams of travel to dead worlds while Earth was so full of troubles.

But there was still a fever to explore the unknown, to bend technology into extensions of man. In 1965 there were even "aquanauts" exploring the ocean depths—"The Next U.S. Frontier," as *Life* put it in a report on the 1965 *Sealab* underwater research project off the California coast near San Diego. In fact, Scott Carpenter, who in 1963 was the second U.S. astronaut to make an orbital flight, headed that *Sealab* mission, which stayed 200 feet underwater for a record-breaking thirty days.[2]

"Today, in outer space, and in aquanaut searches of the sea, we are discovering climates potentially habitable to man, scarcely dreamed of in our past," wrote CBS News anchor Walter Cronkite in an article anticipating the imminent Moon landing.[3]

The path to the Moon had followed the scenario envisioned by *Mercury* astronaut Gordon Cooper during the early Space Age. "The first manned shot is going to be a ballistic firing; that is, the man will be fired off from

Canaveral, go about 100 miles up, float there weightless in the capsule for a few minutes and then come back down into the Atlantic on a ballistic trajectory," Cooper explained in the first of the special *Life* articles on the Moon race. "We're just getting started here with space programs that will continue as long as man can pick himself up and go. And there will be a lot of firsts: the first man on a ballistic firing, the first man into orbit, the first man to orbit the Moon, the first man to land on the moon."[4]

Then came the day when it finally happened.

Astronaut Neil Armstrong reached the bottom rung of the ladder leading from the *Apollo 11 Eagle* module to the lunar surface, and a global television audience was watching it all. While descending from the lunar module (LM), Armstrong had pulled a lanyard releasing a folded-down compartment that deployed a black-and-white television camera. A radio also broadcast the astronaut's immortal words: "That's one small step for man, one giant leap for mankind."

It required only 1.3 seconds for the image and sound, transmitted from an antenna on the lunar module, to travel the 238,000 miles through space to three receiving stations (in the Mojave Desert, Australia, and Spain), from which the broadcast signal was bounced to the Manned Spacecraft Center in Houston and then relayed to the commercial television networks for transmission to home screens.

After picking up a rock sample (the first order of business in case the mission had to be cut short), the TV camera and a tripod were then set up some fifty feet from the spacecraft. The television images provided earthlings with a live, panoramic view of the barren surface, the first images physically transmitted by a man from the surface of another world. "It's like much of the high desert of the United States," Armstrong remarked. "It's different but it's very pretty out here."

As *New York Times* space reporter John Noble Wilford wrote in his book *We Reach the Moon*: "It was an eerie scene, like a throwback to Buck Rogers science fiction. The black-and-white TV pictures of the bug-shaped Lunar Module and the astronauts were so sharp and clear as to seem unreal, more like a toy and toylike figures than human beings on the most daring and far-reaching expedition thus far undertaken."[5]

The TV broadcasts had actually begun three-quarters of the way to the Moon, with Armstrong and Edwin Aldrin opening a hatch at the top of the mission command ship *Columbia* and squeezing through a narrow tunnel leading to the *Eagle* lunar module. From there the duo provided a televised tour of the vehicle that would be making the lunar descent while Michael Collins kept the command module in orbit.

The *Apollo 11* mission marked not only a historic event in human history, but of the television medium itself. "This combination of the television camera, which does not lie, and the Age of *Apollo* seems to me the most dramatic coupling of events in man's history," Cronkite observed.[6]

While TV transmissions from space began in 1968 with *Apollo 7*, network coverage still depended on simulated animation to give audiences a visual take on a particular mission. Ralph McQuarrie was one of those space flight simulation artists, working on *Apollo* flights for CBS News Special Events from 1965 to 1968. Previously McQuarrie had been illustrating aircraft and

In 1969, this TV Guide issue for July 19–25 was full of articles and programming notes on the anticipated Moon landing. Not only would it be the greatest feat of exploration in human history, television transmissions from the Moon would allow a global audience to bear eyewitness.

Three different animation cel views of Apollo LM prepared by Ralph McQuarrie for use with starfield or lunar surface backgrounds circa 1967 for CBS News Special Events.

aerospace projects at Boeing before moving to Los Angeles, where he was hired by the network.

A decade later McQuarrie would gain renown as the production illustrator on *Star Wars*. McQuarrie, taking George Lucas's direction, would conjure up the look for everything from alien worlds to Luke Skywalker, Darth Vader, the 'droids, and the other *Star Wars* characters. McQuarrie, who had met with Lucas when the filmmaker was looking for concept artists, recalls that Lucas particularly liked a painting he'd done depicting American astronauts greeting a group of fur-covered aliens on a grassy alien world.

But McQuarrie was depicting space travel for real during those Space Race days at CBS. In that pre-computer graphics era, McQuarrie and other simulation artists used old-fashioned cel animation, hard data research, and their imaginations to be the eyes of the TV audience, conveying what the mission might truly look like from any select vantage point in outer space.

"For reference we'd get models of the spacecraft from which I'd make photographs and then make a painting that could serve as an animation cel," McQuarrie recalls. "We'd also be given the flight plan, this big telephone-book thing, so we could determine what the exact position the spacecraft would be at any particular time. We knew the sun's position and what the lighting would have to be like at any point. The director of the show would cut in with what footage was needed to cover a specific thing; it was all predetermined. You had this viewpoint that was unavailable to anyone at the time. It was like a movie."

Simple animation techniques illustrated exactly what the ship was expected to be doing in outer space. "We could rotate the camera to get the images to turn and we could fire the rockets by putting down a rocket flame cel cycle so it'd appear that the rocket was firing," McQuarrie says. "We could make it look like our spacecraft was dropping into space by moving the camera back and holding the background so it'd appear to get smaller or larger. All simple animation, but it looked pretty good. Nowadays it's far more sophisticated, far better, with a computer that can be programmed to rotate a three-dimensional image into any position, allow lighting changes, and whatever you want.

"It was a thrill to see my work on television. I remember one time [astronaut] Wally Schirra was providing commentary with Walter Cronkite. It was during a boring stretch on one of the *Apollo* missions, the ship was in orbit on the dark side of the Moon and out of contact, and they were thinking of things to say. So they were broadcasting my animation showing the craft on the dark side of the Moon, with the rocket firing, and so forth. Schirra commented on the animation as being rather good, a particularly nice-looking shot."

McQuarrie, who was living in Los Angeles at the time of the *Apollo 11* landing, recalled how clear it was that historic night. People throughout the world went to their open windows or stood outside in the moonlight contemplating the wonder of it all—there were human beings up there walking around!

Rick McCallum, a film and television producer whose busy 1997 included overseeing the twentieth anniversary *Star Wars Trilogy Special Edition* theatrical rerelease and beginning production work in England on the next chapters in the *Star Wars* series, was fifteen when man first walked on the Moon. McCallum remembers it as one of the seminal events of his young life. "In terms of my life there've been very few times that history forced me to make some kind of decision—I was even too young for Vietnam. What happens with a historic event is you become swept up in a collective world of mass feelings. The assassination of President Kennedy was a big event because that was the first time I realized the world wasn't perfect. But the Moon landing was the biggest for me personally."

McCallum kept vigil the night of the Moon landing in an exotic fairy tale location—the ornate Neuschwanstein Castle in Bavaria, built in the mid–nineteenth century by the "Mad King" Ludwig II. "I was with my mother and a gathering of people on the bottom level of the castle," McCallum recalls. "This castle is just a magical, extraordinary place set against these breathtaking snowcapped mountains. We didn't even watch the Moon walk on television, we listened to it on the radio. It was a BBC broadcast and I forget who the announcer was, but he was so emotional, which was very unlike the British. But in this extraordinary setting we could see all the stars—it was almost like we could see Neil and the boys landing! I remember going out into the village the next morning and being so proud to be American. People came up and were shaking my hand and rubbing my hair. A very amazing moment. Then I went to Munich about three days later and the awe that people still had was just phenomenal.

"Listening to the radio broadcast of the Moon landing, I believed there was nothing we couldn't do collectively. It's been deeply disappointing to me that we haven't gone back out into space—politics and money, that's what it's all about. I find among my own kids and young people in general a *major* desire to travel in space. Kids are really interested in the idea that there's somebody else out there. Some people wake up when they're thirteen or fourteen years old and ask, 'Who am I? Why am I here?' For two thousand years that has been our tradition. But it's only been in the last thirty to forty years where people can also say—*I want to go there!* To literally find a new world."

(ABOVE LEFT) *Edwin Aldrin, lunar module pilot and second man to walk on the Moon, is photographed by Neil Armstrong during Extravehicular Activity (EVA) in the Sea of Tranquility. Behind Aldrin is the lunar module, to his right the already deployed Solar Wind Composition experiment. While Aldrin and Armstrong were on the surface, command module pilot Michael Collins kept the command and service modules in a lunar orbit. (ABOVE) One of the giant steps left on the lunar surface. (Photos courtesy of NASA.)*

The Apollo 11 *moon landing was a celebration for all the peoples of Earth— as seen in these international stamps honoring the historic event and the NASA space program.*

Jonathan Harris has recalled the fun he had dreaming up wry digs and lusty invectives to toss against the Robot (animated by Bob May, with voice by Dick Tufeld). In this scene Smith, who once created a painting he dubbed portrait of the "inner feelings of the sensitive man in space," seems to be debating the finer points of art with his "bubble-headed" antagonist.

⑦ ROBOT LOVE

> *I compute you well.*
>
> **—THE ROBOT TO WILL ROBINSON IN "WAR OF THE ROBOTS,"**
> **LOST IN SPACE *EPISODE TWENTY, SEASON ONE***

ne of the great early sideshows of *Lost in Space* was Will and Dr. Smith's tug of war over the Robot. While sabotaging the *Jupiter 2* mission, Smith, a proclaimed cybernetics master, had wired the environmental control robot to obey only his voice commands. But Will discovered that by mimicking Zachary's voice, he could assert command control over the Robot.

Eventually the Robot would be rewired and become like one of the family—and a source of chagrin to a continually vexed Smith. Whether playing an acoustic guitar or donning a chef's hat and apron to bake a cake, the Robot was seemingly reprogrammed, as Will once put it, for "sentimental stuff." One of the campy highlights of the infamous "The Great Vegetable Rebellion" episode was a birthday party for the Robot: "When I told him, he practically broke his power pack with embarrassment," said Judy of the Robot's reaction to the birthday news.

WAR OF THE ROBOTS

A classic Robot episode was "War of the Robots," which co-starred the robotic rival Robby, already a movie star and robot icon from such films as *Forbidden Planet* (MGM, 1956) and *The Invisible Boy* (MGM, 1957).

In the "War," Robby the Robot played a "robotoid," a machine with free choice. Discovered rusted and seemingly abandoned, the robotoid threw our Robot into a suspiciously human fit of jealousy as he cried out: "My sensors will not accept the possibility of its existence!"

The Robot repeatedly warned Will not to awaken the sleeper, but our young hero brought the robotoid back to life. The robotoid began to supplant Robot in providing expert service to the Robinson camp, with fickle Dr. Smith among the first to turn his back on his former mechanical cohort.

"You are obviously of a very primitive design," the robotoid said when he finally confronted the Robot.

"The Robinsons belong to me," Robot proclaimed. "I will not give up my family."

The superior robotoid hit an overmatched Robot with an electrical charge. Finally, feeling obsolete, Robot wandered off to overload his power cells and burn out his primary memory banks. Will, missing his robot friend, found the mechanical creation still functioning, the circuit breakers preventing his "suicide."

Unknown to the *Jupiter 2* camp, the robotoid was actually paving the way for his alien masters to capture the Robinsons and begin human experiments. In the end our Robot used guile and strategy to defeat the robotoid and reclaim his position as part of the family and crew of the *Jupiter 2*.

(ABOVE) *Lineup of classic robot toys (with a host of Robbys). Can you find the* Lost *Robot? (From the collection of Bob Burns; photo by Bruce Walters.)* (OPPOSITE) *For the 1998* Lost in Space *movie, the Robot would undergo a major transformation, first as an imposing "evil" Robot at the service of Dr. Smith . . .* (TOP INSET). *. . . then transformed into a form both pleasing and familiar* (BOTTOM INSET). *(Production stills by Milly Donaghy, New Line Cinema.)* (TOP) *Robot awaits as director Stephen Hopkins and Gary Oldman (Dr. Smith) confer on set.* (BOTTOM) *Matt LeBlanc (Don West) with Robot.*

THE ART OF ANIMATRONICS

In late July 1997 the Honda Motor Company released photos through Associated Press showing "P-2," a six-foot-tall, battery-powered robot whose design mimicked the human form, walking up stairs under its own power.

Once the stuff of science fiction, robots in all their varied incarnations and forms are part of our modern technological landscape, made possible by the increasing miniaturization of electronics and mechanics. Automated bank teller machines, telephone answering machines, and even solar-powered, self-steering lawnmowers are everyday robots. Industrial uses range from assembly-line robotic arms welding auto bodies to remote devices that can enter nuclear-radiated areas and other disaster zones (or even scuttle into an Alaskan volcano, like NASA's ten-foot-tall, eight-legged spider "Dante," a robot explorer with video camera eyes which in 1994 was controlled by technicians thousands of miles away while viewing the robot via satellite).[1]

In the entertainment industry, robotics technologies not only bring robot characters to life, but imitate life-forms in all their organic glory, unlike the old costume suits that realized the female robot of 1926's *Metropolis*, the 'droids of *Star Wars*, Robby, Robot, and others.

Visual effects artist Stan Winston hails the new "symbiotic relationship" between robotics technology and the creation of art. Winston is one of the world's experts in animatronics, the craft of creating and controlling a puppet creation through electronics, mechanical cables, or radio control. (These creations can also be creature suits, although new technologies allow for cable or remote control to animate various aspects of such wonder suits.) The Stan Winston Studio (headquartered in Van Nuys, California) has produced not merely anima-

BOB MAY

Bob May is resplendent in a bright blue jacket, dress pants, white shirt, and red tie, holding court at Supercon II, a 1997 comic book and fantasy convention being held in an Oakland, California, hotel. May would make the perfect incarnation of the man-behind-the-curtain in a *Wizard of Oz* movie remake, but he'd be the kind of wizard who'd probably spare poor Dorothy the trouble of dispatching evil witches and go straight to the click-your-heels-for-home trick.

At his Supercon II table, May greets a steady stream of *Lost in Space* fans who ask for an autograph, snap a photograph, or tell him of happy childhood memories of the show ("The Robot was my favorite character," gushes one female fan). May offers up his high-energy, enthusiastic self, answering the inevitable Robot questions as if for the first time: "Did it get hot in there?" asks one fan. "My own private sauna," May responds without missing a beat.

Perhaps less known, even by *Lost in Space* fans, is that May is a true trouper, hailing from an old showbiz family (his grandfather was Chic Johnson of the "Hellzapoppin'" comedy team of Olsen and Johnson). May's career, which began in 1941 at the age of two, has extended from the twilight of New York's vaudeville stages to the soundstages and back lots of Hollywood (including dancing in *Jailhouse Rock* and performing in nine Jerry Lewis movies). He repeats, with conviction, his personal mantra: "I'm so thankful I'm in a business I love and getting paid for it."

On two of his fingers he wears the rings that hearken back to classic showbiz traditions: one a "king of comedy" ring made specially for, and handed down from, his beloved late father; the other a ring carved with the figure of an elephant with its trunk up ("That's very good luck in my business").

It's to May's credit that he's managed to emerge from the shadow—make that the metal encasing—of *Lost*'s Robot. All the performance aspects of the Robot were May's own. So how the heck did he manage to make the Robot rotate three hundred sixty degrees? "That was my little trick," May says with a wink, "and I'm going to take it to the grave. If I revealed that, everyone would know how to do it. My grandson is nine-and-a-half months old and he ain't going to take over the Robot from me—I still like doing the job!"

May takes a break from the convention to head out into the Bay Area sunshine for a smoke and some "I, Robot" memories. Although he reflects on the curious fact that he was never seen in his most famous role, people know it now. In promotional material for the many celebrity party cruises he hosts, he even headlines himself as "Bob May the Robot."

People think the Robot was real! That was Irwin's concept. At the time it probably hurt me as an actor that I was inside the Robot and nobody knew it, although now they know worldwide. An actor takes pride in what he does, but Irwin was right. Nowadays I think we tell too much about how things are done, which takes the mystery away.

But I never thought of the Robot as a piece of equipment. It was my costume. The Robot would react as I would as an actor. You develop a personality with a continuing character. You build that characterization, but you can't rush it because no personality grows overnight. In the series, the Robot was originally a piece of machinery, programmed for the mission then reprogrammed by Dr. Smith to do the sabotaging that got us lost in space. Then Will Robinson reprogrammed the robot again. The Robot had a love for the family, a friendship with Will, and there was the craziness with Dr. Smith—those two were like the greatest comedy team ever. So, those combinations will build a character very fast.

In the first episode, the Robot actually walked, but I got cut up so bad I made every Halloween haunted house with bloody bodies look sane! There was blood coming from everywhere. Inside I was wearing heavy stuff to protect me, but that doesn't matter when you're talking about metal. I looked at the producer, the producer looked at me, and he said, "I think we'd better straighten this out." So usually they'd pull me on cables.

Once when I was in the Robot and being pulled up into the spaceship by this cable pulley system, somebody stepped on the cable. It worked like a slingshot shooting me up into the air. I did a three-sixty—in Olympics terms it was a "ten." When I was in the air, I ducked my head down and pulled my arms in, otherwise I'd have busted my neck and arms. But I was out cold. When I regained conciousness, everybody was concerned about me but not really pleased with my attitude. They're asking, "How are you, Bob?" And I was saying, "How is the Robot?" There's a very simple reason for that—without the Robot I'm out of a job!

I had to be locked into the Robot so that if I spun around it wouldn't come apart. One day, everyone on the **Lost in Space** set broke for lunch and as a practical joke Bill Mumy and Mark Goddard told the prop guys not to let me out. So I'm inside the Robot and I lit up a cigarette. Now, I'm not advocating smoking, but I do smoke. So Irwin Allen comes on the set, sees smoke coming out of the robot, and runs for a fire extinguisher! And I said, "No, Mr. Allen, it's only me." It was my downfall, actually, because he told Stu Moody, our special effects man, that anytime we had to have smoke coming out of the Robot "hand Bob a cigar!"

I'm in a business that I love. I've been having fun since I was two years old. I've been on Broadway; I was in the last of vaudeville, following Judy Garland's show into the Palace Theater in New York. I've done live television in New York with my family and have been in feature films. I was a singer, a dancer, and I did stunts for a while. I just love the business.

Right now I'm putting together a big musical-comedy vaudeville review, taking some one hundred fifty people on the road. I'm producing it, directing it, and I'm one of the stars. We'll do about sixteen cities in twenty weeks. We're going to have vaude-ville acts, chorus lines with show girls, and a twenty-piece orchestra. It's bringing back vaudeville entertainment the way I remember it.

Back in the old vaudeville days there was a bond between performers. People helped each other. To a certain degree you have that today, but some performers have attitudes. I look at them and I think about all the greatness and fun and learning they're missing. A true performer goes out to perform and remembers the word **entertainment**. That's what this business is all about. Be humble and happy and count your blessings. I was just raised right for this business. **Respect** and **gratitude** are big words in my vocabulary.

Bob May emerges from the confines of the Robot.

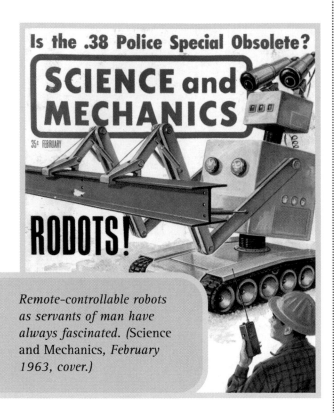

Is the .38 Police Special Obsolete?

SCIENCE and MECHANICS

35¢ FEBRUARY

RODOTS!

Remote-controllable robots as servants of man have always fascinated. (Science and Mechanics, *February 1963, cover.*)

tronics effects but *characters*, including the deep-space creatures of *Aliens* (1986), the alien warrior of *Predator* (1987), and the mechanical dinosaurs that complemented ILM's computer graphics dinosaurs in *Jurassic Park* (1993) and its 1997 sequel, *The Lost World.*

"Art is constantly pushing technology, technology is constantly pushing art," Winston observes. "The Robot of *Lost in Space* or Robby was based on things actually happening in the scientific world, the utilitarian robots being developed. Now you have things like our *Lost World* dinosaurs that require robotics which are *more* sophisticated than those in the aerospace industry. There's still a need for a utilitarian robot, as we saw so dramatically in the Pathfinder landing on Mars. But if you take that utilitarian robot and put it next to one of the robots we've had to develop, ours are far more intricate and involved. That's not to diminish in any way the breakthroughs of our probes and robotics going into outer space, but inherent in them is a simplicity of design, while our robots are not supposed to be robots! We're simulating life, which presents a different set of problems.

"We have aerospace engineers and machinists

working in our studio who want to tell stories with technology. We're advancing the artistic world by telling stories, simulating animals and human beings, which requires multifunction and organic movement, an extreme number of compound moves that have to be coordinated and finessed. I'm talking specifically about something as powerful and dramatic as the T-rex we created for *Lost World.* That particular robot weighed nine tons and was powerful enough to literally rip the roof off of a car, yet accurate and finessed enough to grab hold of an actor and pull him out of that car without killing him, while also having enough points of motion to look like a real animal."

The early generations of animatronics creations often resembled glorified mechanical puppets, with off-camera "puppeteers" operating hidden cables controlling hydraulics systems. Robotics technologies circa 1997 now allow for self-contained creations that can be operated exclusively with radio signals. "We've advanced far beyond what most people would understand as robotics," Winston says. "We're incorporating computers in the design of all our robots. The use of computers is one of the reasons we've been able to advance our robots to the level we have."

Winston foresees the robotics evolution incorporating ever more sophisticated computers with advanced signals allowing ever finer control and consequently more realistic organic movement. "The only way we can foresee the future is to look to the developments of the past," Winston concludes. "The developments of this century are mind-boggling. We've learned to fly, we've created television, we've gone to the Moon, we've sent a robot to Mars. You've never seen anything from a technological standpoint stand still. Our field is just another element of technical and scientific advancement, it's just driven by the artistic world. So whatever we can't do today, we'll strive to do tomorrow."

ROBOTS IN SPACE: 1997

> *Robot probes no bigger than bacteria will eventually be possible. According to K. Eric Drexler, author of* Engines of Creation, *they will use nanotechnology to assemble devices atom by atom or molecule by molecule . . . a bundle of nanorobots would be the perfect interstellar emissaries.*
>
> **—DENNIS OVERBYE, "IS ANYBODY OUT THERE?"**
> **TIME *SPECIAL ISSUE*: BEYOND THE YEAR 2000, FALL 1992**

One of the concerns for future manned space explorations is that the seemingly infinite vastness of space makes it problematic, if not impossible, for mortals to venture too far beyond the solar system. Robots could be our surrogates into the deepest reaches of space, or pave the way by being launched to specific planets to set up colonies in anticipation of later human arrivals. A former Soviet cosmonaut named Konstantin Feoktistov has even proposed combining robots with a kind of "human fax." As a *Time* article explains:

Feoktistov has pointed out that it might be possible to someday "download" the entire contents of a human brain into a computer, the way a file on a PC can be transferred onto a floppy disk, and broadcast it to a robot in a remote star system. After a few days or years of exposure to this strange world, the surrogate brain would "fax" its new information back to earth and its original owner.[2]

The year 1997 had its own wonders, such as the Mars Pathfinder mission, which landed the first remote-controllable robot emissary on another world. It was the most significant probe to Mars since NASA launched *Viking 1* and *2* in 1975. "The *Viking* landings were like two picnic tables that set down on Mars," explains Roger Gilbertson, president of Mondo-tronics, a northern California company specializing in hobby robotics. "They each had a long mechanical scoop arm that reached out and scooped up dirt and dropped them into a chemical lab to do tests. We've sent other things to Mars, like the Mars *Observer* [launched September 25, 1992], but the final autopsy I heard was that a valve failed and the fuel exploded in the tubing, not the engine, and it blew up when it was in a Martian orbit."

The *Observer* disaster came at a turning point in NASA thinking. Previously, NASA projects required "space-qualified" technologies that had already flown in space, a policy that throttled new technologies. When NASA administrator Daniel Goldin took over the agency in 1992, it was decided that instead of the billion-dollar NASA projects of old, which took years to unfold, the new NASA would emphasize launching many cost-effective missions over shorter periods of time.

The sun as viewed from Mars (thanks to the transmissions from the Mars Pathfinder/Sojourner mission).

Gilbertson himself was part of this new NASA effort, helping bring to the space agency's attention a new type of wire perfect for unmanned space probes and other missions. This breakthrough "shape memory alloy" (which Gilbertson has also dubbed "muscle wire") was an actuator, a device for receiving electrical or thermal energy and transforming it into controllable motion, and was utilized in Pathfinder's *Sojourner*, the foot-tall, two-foot long, six-wheeled robot on Mars. Leading the approval process was Geoffrey Landis at the NASA Lewis Research Center in Cleveland, Ohio, which proved to NASA that the wire would work, subjecting it to the temperature stresses the material would face on the alien world.

While the *Sojourner* robot slowly moved around the Martian surface, a tiny strip of muscle wire (half a business card in length, according to Gilbertson) would receive a remote-controlled signal from Earth and pivot open a glass slide on the robot's solar panel deck, allowing a sensor to measure dust and climate conditions. "We sent NASA our stock wire, the stuff I would ship to any hobbyist in their home," Gilbertson says.

The wire is basically composed of thin, highly processed strands of a nickel-titanium shape memory alloy that can assume different shapes at different temperatures. Gilbertson describes its abilities in his book *Muscle Wires Project Book*, citing an example using two AA batteries to power a length of wire so it could contract and lift a weighted lever: "Pressing the switch lets power flow from the batteries through the Muscle Wire, heating it and causing it to contract and raise the lever and lift the weight. When power is removed, the Muscle Wire cools and relaxes, and the weight helps it return to its starting position."

The shape memory alloy was originally developed in 1932 and made of gold and cadmium, a very toxic material, according to Gilbertson. In 1965 the Navy got a patent on a nickel-titanium shape memory alloy. It was in the early seventies that Gilbertson came into the picture, having become familiar with the shape memory alloy while working at Raychem in Menlo Park, California (where the wire was used in aircraft designs and other applications). Then, in 1985 at the Future World Expo held in San Francisco, Gilbertson met Wayne Brown, the American representative of Toki, a Japanese company that had been developing the wire for use in surgical equipment and implants (thanks to the alloy's "bio-compatibility"). Brown would eventually start his own company built around applications of the shape memory alloy, and become a key supplier to Gilbertson's Mondo-tronics company—and ultimately NASA's Pathfinder mission.

But before the NASA breakthrough, Gilbertson and his partner Chris Paine had been conducting their own research into the wire, even using it to power window displays and the like (such as a collection of robot beetles and butterflies at the Smithsonian Insect Museum). In 1994, during a conference in New York City co-sponsored by NASA and the Planetary Society, Gilbertson brought the wire to the space agency's attention through his presentation of a paper titled "A Survey of Micro-Actuator Technologies for Future Spacecraft Missions."

Gilbertson's paper (the outgrowth of brainstorming sessions with John Busch, another partner) identified ten basic actuators concerned with transforming energy into motion. "I'm not a Ph.D. or a researcher, but I can get into a subject and put things in order," Gilbertson says. "At the talk I basically outlined the tool kit. The jumping-off point was the muscle wire, the shape-changing alloy which I'd been working with the previous six years."

As Gilbertson's paper explained:

The requirements for new types of spacecraft destined to travel throughout our solar system and beyond require examination of the full range of these new actuation and control methods, to focus on those having appropriate performance, efficiency, and size. Designers of future spacecraft must consider those new MEMS [micro-electro-mechanical systems] technologies, which will play key roles in future electronic and mechanical spacecraft components. . . .

Sojourner *on Mars, 1997.*
(Photo courtesy of NASA.)

An actuator's work output density, or work output per unit volume, provides a key measure for comparing various actuator technologies. Reducing spacecraft mass directly lowers the launch costs, hence the overall mission price. . . . Therefore, technologies which perform more work with less mass have great economic value.[3]

"The shape memory alloy wire is not as efficient as a motor," Gilbertson notes, "but a motor is going to weigh 5,000 times what the wire will weigh for the same amount of movement. And the wire will be able to go for millions and millions of cycles. And when you're going to the stars you need a lot of speed, and the less energy you need the more affordable the mission is. Shape memory alloys, out of all the actuators we surveyed, have the highest force for their unit weight. It's the smallest, strongest way to make things move."

Having played a role in the creation of a device that extended humankind's reach millions of miles from Earth is gratifying for Gilbertson, who was eight years old when he thrilled to the television images of the first Moon walk. "The instrument did some very nice science in a very simple and elegant way—which was the point of that conference in New York," Gilbertson says, smiling.

ROBOT WARS

*Mild-mannered software engineers at work,
they were turned manic by the din of crushing metal.*

**—DESCRIPTION OF TWO APPRECIATIVE ROBOT WARS SPECTATORS IN
"ROBOT-FIGHTING CONTEST DRAWS AGGRESSIVE TECHIES," BY AURELIO ROJAS,
SAN FRANCISCO CHRONICLE, MONDAY, AUGUST 18, 1997**

The color poster art by Marc Gabbana celebrating the 1997 Robot Wars, the fourth annual clash of remote-controlled robotics creations, was a wish-fulfillment of heavy-metal robot-philes: In a rugged battlefield enclosed by a vast, domed stadium, seemingly gigantic robotic creations armed with deadly, metal-slicing devices squared off under the searchlight beams of a flying machine.

The thrasher action of Robot Wars that unfolded at San Francisco's Fort Mason Center the weekend of August 15, 1997, featured more than 100 robots competing in elimination rounds, finals, and a grand finale free-for-all "Melee Competition." Most had the lawnmower and vacuum-cleaner look of household appliances; others emulated organic forms in their design—the resulting creations were whatever the robot makers could pound and weld together in their shops or garages. All were remote-controlled and armed with spinning blade edges, twirling battering ram devices, cutting saws, or levers to catch and flip opposing robots. All had such no-nonsense nasty names as "Gut Rip," "The Mauler," "Biohazard," "Destructomatic," "Pretty Hate Machine," "Vlad the Impaler," and "No Love."

Under hot lights some 1,300 spectators packed bleachers that ringed three sides of "the Pit," the square battlefield area staked off by clear, eight-and-a-half-foot-tall shielding vital to protecting the flesh of human spectators from any flying chunks of metal. The competition wasn't anything-goes—rules ranged from weight class divisions to a scoring system—but the event had about it a gladiatorial energy as the crowd screamed in pleasure at the roar of the machines and the buzz of the cutting saws. "You can smell it in the air, ladies and gentlemen—that's robotic victory," announcer Joel Hodgson (creator of the *Mystery Science Theater* cable TV series) said as a haze of diesel fumes rose above the Pit during the heat of competition.

The 1997 "Wars" robot makers ranged from electronics and robotics hobbyists to professionals such as animatronics specialist Mark Setrakian, mechanical department head at Cinovation Studios in Los Angeles (the effects shop owned by Academy Award–winning makeup and creature creator Rick Baker). One of the highlights of the 1997 competition was a battle between the Scorpion, a robot shaped like its namesake, and a Setrakian creation dubbed the Snake but that he personally called by the Latin title *Tenebrae*—translated as "shadows and darkness."

"The reason I don't really like the name 'Snake' is because the robot's concept is a modular one and the snake shape is only one of its possible configurations," says Setrakian. "I think of this robot as a research project. Certainly this year it wasn't ready for competition."

Setrakian's recent professional work included building the mechanism, puppeteering, and even supplying the voice for one of the 1997 movie *Men in Black* aliens (dubbed "Chucky," a tiny being that operated within a human form from a "control room" inside the skull). In between his professional obligations, Setrakian and a three-person L.A. crew rushed their robotic creation to completion in twelve days, just in time to drive the robot up north to the San Francisco competition.

Although his robot would be pinned and lose to the Scorpion, Setrakian did win a trophy for "Strangest Robot." The Snake was able to move almost organically, slinking forward, writhing, opening its jaws, and moving its tail (complete with a hammer drill at the end) in response to Setrakian's radio-controlled puppeteering. Snake/*Tenebrae* was Setrakian's vision of future robots that would advance the form beyond ordinary "lawn-mower" or "weed-whacker" designs. "People come to Robot Wars to see strange robots," he notes. "I'd like to see more creative designs, and a little less wheeled vehicles with drills strapped on. Those are the kinds of robots that can be built by hobbyists without spending too much time or money. Something like the Snake is deceptively complicated and takes a lot of resources.

"There are companies making serious robots, but very few of them are engaged in Robot Wars," Setrakian adds. "In 1995 there was an entry from a company called Schilling Robotics, which makes serious robotic limbs for nuclear reactors, submersible vehicles, and military applications. They called their robot 'Thor,' and it was a very strong robot. They basically utilized the technology they were familiar with, using a lot of titanium and military supply hydraulics valves. In my professional work I basically make mechanical creatures, so with my robots I'm bringing in the technologies I'm familiar with."

Although Setrakian's Cinovation creations are seen by millions of moviegoers on the big screen, TV, and video, his work is always part of a team effort. To him, nothing beats the thrill of building his own mechanical remote-controlled creation and unleashing it in a mechanical mano a mano. "I really enjoy bringing something that turns the crowd on, that gets them excited," Setrakian smiles. "In a way, as a Robot Wars contestant you're in a very strange and tiny wing of the entertainment industry. You're building something and bringing it to delight a crowd which is right there and gives you direct feedback.

"There's a strange feeling you get when you send your robot into the arena. Here's something you've spent weeks, perhaps months, building. You've spent a lot of money. And now you're going to send it into the arena and somebody is going to try to destroy it! There's this pressure and anxiety and then it's all over. I imagine that's the way athletes like boxers or Olympic sprinters must feel.

"Going into the arena to fight the Scorpion, my robot was really being turned on for the first time. It got a bit of a whack from the [robotic tail] of the Scorpion, but that was easily fixed. One of the things that went wrong was the motors for the jaws are so powerful that the amperes they were drawing from the batteries caused the switch that drove the jaws within the robot to actually melt down. But I'm happy to say the Scorpion guys were so cool, they helped me reweld and basically get it together for the rest of the weekend. And even though the jaws didn't work during the Melee competition, it did roll across the arena and wrap itself around one robot, hold it, and even drill into it with a hammer drill built at one end."

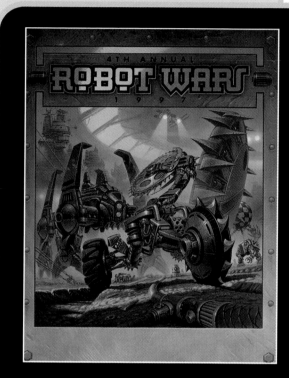

High-tech carnage aplenty is promised in this Marc Gabbana poster art advertising the 1997 Robot Wars competition. (©Marc Gabbana)

DICK TUFELD

While some original *Lost in Space* cast members agreed to participate in the big-budget *Lost in Space* movie during the shoot at Shepperton Studios in England (with cameo appearances by June Lockhart, Angela Cartwright, Marta Kristen, and an extended scene played by Mark Goddard), Dick Tufeld was the only classic cast member to play his old character—all he needed was the power of his voice.

Back in the *Lost* TV days, it was Tufeld who memorably dubbed in the Robot's mechanical voice to complement Bob May's performances within the metal suit. In the *Lost in Space* movie, Tufeld provides menacing intonations for a new, evil Robot commanded by Dr. Smith. When the Robot is destroyed and rebuilt by Will, Tufeld's voice provides the kinder, gentler (and more familiar) voice for the resurrected Robot. Tufeld's voice has also been used in a line of classic and movie tie-in Robot toys, his mechanical tones ready to dig into the consciousness of a new generation.

It's a voice that plucks at the memory strings whenever Tufeld is introduced as "the voice of the Robot from *Lost in Space*." Whether being introduced to a waitress at a restaurant in Sydney, Australia (where he'd gone with Bob May in March 1996 as part of a gala "Robinson Robot Body and Soul Tour"), or to an all-American linebacker visiting Tufeld's home town of Pasadena, California, for a recent pre–Rose Bowl fete, the response is usually the same—the individual rings out in imitation of the famous Robot lines: "Warning, Warning!" and "Danger, Will Robinson!" Although he's accustomed to it by now, it's a reaction that still astounds Tufeld.

Tufeld's career as an announcer and voice performer began with a boyhood fascination with the entrancing sounds that emanated from the speakers of his home radio set. It was the golden age of the medium, an era when radio was a theater of the mind, broadcasting not only the requisite news, sports, music, and talk fests still popular today, but variety shows, dramas, comedies, and more.

"I listened to *The Shadow*, *The Green Hornet*, *The Lone Ranger*, *Superman*—you name it," Tufeld explains with a smile. "It was such a wonderful art form. There's nothing as vivid as the imagination. Nowadays they don't even have the kind of announcing they had back then, like on *The Lone Ranger*. The 'William Tell Overture' would strike up, there'd be the sound of gunfire, and the announcer would describe a fiery horse with a speed of light, a cloud of dust, and a hearty 'Hi Ho Silver! . . . the Lone Ranger rides again!' You'd hear the hoof beats of Silver and then the Lone Ranger shouting, 'Come on, Silver, let's go big fella.' As a kid it was very exciting."

The seeds of Tufeld's eventual involvement with *Lost in Space* were planted back in 1945 during his stint at Hollywood radio station KLAC, where he engineered and spun the theme music for a showbiz gossip program hosted by future television and movie producer Irwin Allen. There was an age difference between the two (Tufeld was in his late teens and Allen, then a literary agent, was in his thirties), which Tufeld thinks explains their literally nodding acquaintance. "He'd walk in and nod to me; then nod when he left," Tufeld recalls. Years later, when Allen was looking for an announcer for the *Lost in Space* series he was preparing, Tufeld was recommended by a friend who worked at Fox. "'How about Dick Tufeld?' my friend said to Allen," Tufeld recalls. "'Dick Tufeld! My oldest and dearest friend,' Irwin said. Astonishing."

When a Robot voice-over was needed, Allen gave Tufeld a crack at the job. The two met at the Fox looping room for the audition, with Tufeld offering to create a robotic, mechanical voice. "My dear fellow," is how Tufeld recalls Allen's reply, "this is a highly advanced civilization. I want a cultured Robot."

Tufeld took the script and, in the mellifluous manner of legendary radio voice Alexander Scourby, read: "Warning! Danger, Will Robinson." After ten minutes, Allen waved the session to a close. "You're not getting it," the producer complained. But Tufeld asked Allen if he could give it one more try. Then he read his lines in the mechanical manner he'd first offered to perform. "'My God!' Irwin says. 'That's what I was looking for all the time! What the hell took you so long?' I had to turn my back on him for a moment because I nearly burst out laughing."

The first time I realized the character of the Robot had great significance to people was around 1976 when I was invited to speak to a TV production class at Syracuse University. The professor had asked me for a list of my TV credits, so I'd listed the news and sports anchor work I'd done, network and commercial announcing, as well as announcing for the ABC **Movie of the Week,** the Emmys and Grammys, and programs like the **Tom Jones** show. It was a long list and the last credit mentioned was that I'd been the voice of the Robot from **Lost in Space.** While this professor was introducing me, the class was pretty quiet—until he read the final part about my involvement in **Lost in Space.** Then a murmur went up, the students began excitedly looking at each other, then applauding. I was astonished!

Neither Bob May or myself got cast credit at the end of each episode of the TV show because Irwin wanted people to believe that this was a real robot. And it worked! I've talked to many people who watched the show as kids and never realized that there was somebody inside the Robot.

For me there wasn't anything very creative about doing the Robot's voice since I was locked into Bob's timings. To me it was a technical, mechanical job. Bob May would be inside the Robot and as he spoke the lines, with each syllable he'd press a button inside the claw and the chest circuit lights would flash. I had to be in synch with his voice and the light flashes. I'd go into the looping room at Twentieth Century Fox where they'd run footage of the Robot and I'd watch the screen with my earphones on and speak into a microphone. Actually, some things don't change: The setup was similar to the reading I did for the movie, where, in a well-equipped facility at Shepperton Studio in England, I'd watch the footage on this huge screen while wearing a pair of earphones and reading the lines.

The big difference was instead of me having to be in synch with the Robot, they could synch to me. Just the reverse of the television show. When the movie production began, they'd had me record all the Robot lines to cue the actors on the set. Then, in post-production, I went back to London to do the lines again, this time with heavy interpretation. Director Stephen Hopkins would be there with me, directing me to give a more intense performance.

The energy of the movie is very different from the old TV series. For example, the Dr. Smith played by Jonathan Harris had comedic overtones, while the Smith played by Gary Oldman is dead serious, dark, and brooding. I think a lot of the people who watched the show as kids should see the movie on its own terms, not as a continuation of the original series.

The thing about **Lost in Space** is that two years after it was canceled it went into syndication and it's never been out of syndication since. Somewhere in the world **Lost in Space** is playing. Nowadays, when middle-aged people see the show, they remember their childhoods and growing up. There's a powerful sense of nostalgia.

Dick Tufeld, *voice of the Robot.*

⊟ FUTURE TENSE

The year 1997 envisioned in *Lost in Space* was an analog future of mainframe computers and reel-to-reel tape-recording equipment. Sometimes the technology on board the *Jupiter 2* had the magical quality of those "moving sidewalk" visions of the future—such as Maureen's amazing onboard "environmental computer," which at the press of a button automatically and miraculously produced plastic-wrapped meals.

Of course, the newly imagined space-traveling Robinsons in production for the movies during the *real* 1997 reflected the new *fin de siècle* times. In *LS* there's a cynicism with institutional authority (the people of Earth have been fooled into believing that "recycling technologies" have reversed the depletion of natural resources). In the real-life nineties, with the end of the Cold War and the fracturing of the old Soviet Union, the new threat to the *Jupiter 2* mission (this time headed for the habitable world of Alpha Prime) is the terrorism of the "New Global Sedition," with Dr. Smith as agent saboteur. The voyage to the garden paradise of the "new Eden" is sponsored by the U.S. Army—and the Coca-Cola Corporation.

The new *Jupiter 2* was launched in a world that has technologically recast itself since the sixties, and the movie adventure only slightly stretches the new technoreality: Penny con-cocts her own video journals using a wrist video camera; the ship's computer is able to produce holographic images; Will has the ability to not only hack into the Robot's internal wiring but to implant his own mind and personality within the circuitry.

In the reality of 1997, digital dominates analog, the virtual world of the Internet is still evolving, the nuts and bolts of the machine world have given way to the beginnings of artificial intelligence

THE FUTURE IS NOT WHAT IT USED TO BE.

This Novell ad echoes the way the future was....

THE 21ST CENTURY IS CLOSER THAN YOU THINK.

machines and biotechnology, and the dream of space has settled into the seeming routine of manned orbiting stations and deep space probes.

WEB SIGHTS

Exactly forty years after he sat at his home ham radio set in Los Angeles and heard the beeping pulse of *Sputnik* flying in orbit overhead, Merrill Dean sits in a San Francisco restaurant holding a cellular phone that fits in the palm of his hand. "Soon we'll all be like Dick Tracy with his two-way wrist radio," Dean laughs.

Dean, passing through on a business trip on behalf of IMGIS, a new Internet company for which he is chief operating officer, appreciates the new technological wonderland. But for a lifelong ham enthusiast, it's the proverbial case of déjà vu all over again. "The Internet is essentially the same thing ham radio was, except we're all connected by wires or fiber optics," he notes.

Dean contrasts the miracle of modern global communications with the recent past, in which, due to relatively primitive communications, the world was a much bigger place. "The level of communication in 1967 to 1968 was difficult. I used to handle motion picture and television sales in Latin America for the Walt Disney Company, so I'd travel down there a lot. In some countries you'd have to book hours ahead, sometimes a day, just to make a long-distance phone call to another country. Back then everybody had a telex number on their business card

instead of a fax or, in today's world, an Internet e-mail address. So in a way it's all come full circle.

"Right now the Net is still the Wild West, it's just exploding in connecting everybody worldwide. There's more than fifty million people now in the United States who are getting onto the Internet and I don't know how many websites. Everybody's presence on the Internet is a website and each site is a group of URLs—Uniform Record Locators. For example, Time/Warner's website is 250,000 pages deep and each one of those pages—which can include content from *Time, Fortune, Money*—has its own address, a URL. My company makes deals with individual websites to serve advertising on their particular site [called "banners"]. It's a business that's building very rapidly—today we're delivering 100 million advertisements a month. This technology will make available a lot of information that people never had before and it'll be at their fingertips. People will be able to engage in commerce, make purchases, plan trips, and do research on everything from buying an automobile to making stock purchases."

One corporate player staking a claim on the Internet frontier is Fujitsu Ltd., a $34 billion company that is the world's second-biggest computer maker (after IBM). This international company is spending an estimated half of its $3.6 billion research-and-development budget on Internet and multimedia concerns in the hopes that within a year it will garner a third of its corporate revenues from cyberspace products and services.[1]

By contrast, a comparative pittance of R&D monies—slightly more than $30 million—has been spent on artificial life technologies by Fujitsu Interactive, Inc., the company's interactive multimedia arm, which was incorporated in 1996 and is headquartered in San Francisco. But this research into artificial life technologies and their potential commercial applications has already borne strange fruit. In March 1997 the division released a CD-ROM title that claimed status as the world's first commercially available interactive "virtual companion." Those already convinced that their home computer is possessed by gremlins would be right at home "relationship-building," as Fujitsu Interactive puts it, with Fin Fin, a dolphin-bird creature who lives on the magic planet Teo.

THE BELIEVABLE AGENT

Fin Fin is the pioneer "Believable Agent" Fujitsu Interactive has brought to the marketplace.

According to the Fujitsu division's own corporate statement, "[T]he company is focused on creating virtual beings incorporating Artificial Life technology—that is, autonomous, believable creatures 'living' inside the silicon circuitry of computers—which develops a unique relationship with each user."[2]

Artificial Intelligence (AI), which refers to technologies or systems that can be made to replicate human intelligence factors such as reasoning and cognition, led to Artificial Life (A-Life) research, a decade-old discipline seeking to model ecological and biological processes not observable in nature (allowing, for example, computer models of biological systems to be subjected to programmatic inquiries to see how certain stresses or impacts would unfold over the long timeline of biological evolution).

On the next level are the Believable Agents, which build on both AI and A-Life researches to produce a virtual being designed as a vehicle for multimedia entertainment. "Emotion is the key to the believability of a Believable Agent," explains a Fujitsu Interactive paper on Artificial Life. "Fin Fin's emotional capacity, more than anything else, enables users to achieve the 'suspension of disbelief' and develop a relationship with Fin Fin as though he were a living being. . . .

"Artists are the unmatched masters at building emotion into fictional characters, thereby eliciting the emotional involvement of their audience.

This 1997 Mobil print ad anticipates the International Space Station scheduled to be launched into orbit in 1998.

For this reason, artists have been chosen to lead the way in the efforts of Fujitsu Laboratories to create Believable Agents."[3]

THE TEO PROJECT

By March 1997, Fujitsu Interactive ushered Fin Fin into the marketplace. By fall the company had released an upgraded version of the Teo creature, incorporating a "higher friendliness factor" and featuring additional denizens for the birdlike creature to interact with on his world. One had only to slip in the CD-ROM disc, call up any of the various lush, diverse ecosystems of the planet, and wait for Fin Fin to appear. Shy at first, the hybrid creature reacts to a friendly voice, but has been known to head for cover if the player addresses Fin Fin in an angry tone.

The proprietary technology that produced Fin Fin includes an animation engine for the dolphin-bird's movements and environments, along with audio effects and "real-time" graphics (the company estimates that the virtual creature requires 40,000 polygons—the interconnecting surfaces that form a 3-D image—with more than a million polygons for each planet Teo screen scene). A separate, trademarked "SmartSensor" device allows users to communicate with Fin Fin through words and motions. Ultimately, what makes the Believable Agent animation unfold is its "life engine," which allows Fin Fin to extract sense data stimuli from its world (such as the offering of food by the user or the approach of a Teo sunset), which, combined with its own internal state, such as thirst or fatigue, can lead to any of the possible reflexive and reflective reactions built into the database.

Fin Fin's creative gestation essentially began in 1989, when Fujitsu Laboratories, the R&D center of Fujitsu Ltd., began to explore the AI possibilities of computer-generated creations, an ongoing process the company named the Teo Project. (A cor-

relative, dubbed the "Oz Project," would be the Lab's joint researches with Carnegie-Mellon University to produce interactive characters and artwork incorporating Believable Agents.) The Teo Project leader—or "Visualist," as the company puts it—is Fujitsu Labs' Makoto Tezuka. "I had a passion to create a character," Tezuka has said of Fin Fin, "that would survive for thousands of years."

Digital technologies have not only transformed the visual arts, but allowed the creation of virtual environments—such as Fin Fin's magical world of Teo. (Images supplied by Fujitsu Interactive, Inc.)

FUTURE: DENIED!

> *Cities of Tomorrow: The city of tomorrow, engineers say, will tend first to vastness;*
> *gigantic buildings connected by wide, suspended roadways on which traffic will speed*
> *at unheard-of rates. . . . Helicopter planes, capable of maneuvering about between*
> *buildings and roof-top airports, will take the place of the ground taxi. Each building*
> *will be virtually a city in itself, completely self-sustaining, receiving its supplies from*
> *great merchandise ways far below the ground. . . . Many persons will live in the*
> *healthy atmosphere of the building tops, while others will commute to far distant resi-*
> *dential towns, or country homes.*
>
> **—AMAZING STORIES, AUGUST 1939, BACK COVER TEXT**

That was the City of the Future, conceived in our technological innocence. An April 1942 issue of *Amazing Stories* further posited, "What will the city of tomorrow be like?" and pictured a vast dynamo of a twenty-first-century city, the skies filled with streams of manta ray–shaped flying ships moving above expansive city structures resembling the cathode tube and electronic insides of a TV set, a vision of "plastic, metal, and unbreakable glass . . . of science, of atomic power, of space travel, and of high culture."

In later decades the high hopes of a utopian techno-future began to transmute into prophecies of darkness. In *Time Out of Joint*, written by the late science fiction writer Philip K. Dick and published in 1959, Dick put his character Ragle Gumm into a hallucinatory time warp. The story included a vision of February 1994, the date a battle breaks out on "Base One," a capital of the Moon colonies, during conflicts between space colonists and those who oppose interplanetary travel and rally around the slogan "One Happy World." (The author's predictions hit a little closer to what has come to pass when he imagined a 1998 in which "the kids now talk like and dress like West African natives and the girls wear men's clothing and shave their heads.") [4]

The 1997 imagined in TV's *Lost in Space* was the product of the early post–World War II decades. After the long nightmare of the Depression and the years of global war, the country was enjoying its reward of domestic prosperity and ready to embrace all the comforts that science had been cooking up. The *Jupiter 2*, with its push-button conveniences, robot servant, and high-tech amenities, reflected the still-burning hope for a new world revamped by the wonders of science.

In the postwar years even the promise of "All-Electric Living" was enough to boggle the mind. Electricity is so taken for granted in the nineties (even the inevitable power outages) that it's almost shocking to realize there was a time when electricity was a complete wonder. A 1956 print ad presented by "America's Electric Light and Power Companies" promised a "new electric age" where even "Electricity may be the driver. One day your car may speed along an electric super-highway, its speed and steering automatically controlled by electronic devices embedded in the road. Highways will be made safe—by electricity!" (Of course, forty years later, this concept is still on the table, only computers are imagined to do the job.)

In a September 14, 1959, issue of *Life* magazine (with its cover photo of the seven *Mercury* astronauts), a special thirty-page advertising section publicized model homes wired from the kitchen to the laundry. "I feel so modern," enthused a Mrs. Brown of her new "showcase" electric kitchen. As the supplement noted: "The wire—instead of a fire—is heating, cooking, and drying for [Americans]. . . . The exciting new boom in all-electric living is on."

Certainly the wonders of 1996, with humans technologically extending themselves from cyberspace to outer space, would seem to be fantastic enough. But there were technological promises that haven't been kept. Predictions of an impending superfuture had been drummed into many of the children growing up in the fifties and sixties, who anticipated that in their maturity they would be whisked to work via personal helicopter, there would be robots to handle any messy chores, and it would be possible to take vacations on those inevitable Moon colonies.

"In the sixties we thought that in the future we'd just be able to push a button and things would appear," says Terry Jones, today a researcher for the *Home and Family Show* on the cable Family Channel. "I feel a little cheated. As a kid I thought for sure that by 1997 we'd be traveling on moving sidewalks and flying around in jet packs. By now cars weren't supposed to be using gas, they were supposed to be propelled on cushions of air! Sure we live in the future, but is it accessible to me when I'm walking down the street? Is modern technology really accessible to all of us? To me the future will happen when the scientific breakthroughs show up in our homes."

Mark Moore, of the ILM art department, was born in 1956 and grew up with those same sixties-era dreams of a technowonderland. Moore also poses the question: "What happened to the future?"

"A lot of the things that were supposed to take place as we got to the twenty-first century haven't happened," Moore notes. "I remember in the early sixties, when I was in elementary school, we had a book showing a timeline that had us landing on the Moon in the early seventies, on to Mars by the eighties, then to the solar system and beyond by the year 2000. Some of these things happened; we did get to the Moon and we have unmanned probes to Mars. But I was hoping to see some of the other things everybody back then thought for sure would happen, like domed cities, moving sidewalks, and flying cars."

Moore personally pinpointed 1997 as the year for fulfillment of this technological promise. As a filmmaker, though, Moore is taking steps to set things right: He's working on a ten-to-fifteen-

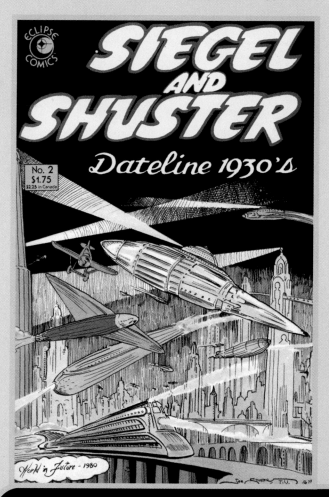

In the 1930s Joe Shuster, who along with writer Jerry Siegel created Superman, imagined the look of the world in the then far-off year of 1980. (Siegel and Shuster: Dateline 1930's, Eclipse Comics publishers, 1985.)

minute short film in which a dimensional traveler uses a 1960 El Camino that transforms into a flying car to zap into the alternate 1997 promised back in the dreamy yesteryear of 1960.

Terry Jones remembers the time her brother came home with an old Buck Rogers ray gun from the thirties, which he'd discovered while exploring the junk piles of an old abandoned house, and how a place of honor was reserved for the futuristic-looking toy. But growing up in Seattle, there were more concrete evidences of the coming future: "As a five-year-old I was overwhelmed by the Space Needle and the Monorail, a Space Age thing which runs on cushions of air," she recalls. "To me this was the future. I had the sense I was getting a glimpse of something."

Jones also grew up on the futuristic dreams celebrated in everything from *Popular Science* magazine and the *Jetsons* animated TV series to science fiction films and the Walt Disney TV show "World of Tomorrow" segments. "I think the difference between when I was a kid and kids today is that we envisioned the future for ourselves," Jones recalls. "When we watched a science fiction film or a TV show like *Lost in Space* we could see the clunkiness, the alien with a zipper up its back. We knew it was fake, but we wanted to believe! Now modern visual effects films are so real everything's envisioned *for* today's kids. I don't know if kids today have that 'Wow!'"

Jones acknowledges that some of the dreams, such as those moving sidewalks, might have been a tad impractical. But she also believed that the first Moon walk heralded a new age. "Hope was the rhythm of the future, that things would always change for the better," she says. "When man walked on the Moon we thought the future had come."

Bill Griffith, the cartoonist mastermind behind the syndicated *Zippy the Pinhead* strip (see the following feature, "Zip Code"), was born in 1944 and borne along on the crest of that first optimistic wave of technological sweet talk. But to Griffith the subtext of the promised future was not about Space Age creature comforts but the corporate takeover of America. "The message was to relax, your house will soon be all-electric or all-plastic, there'll be viewphones and helipads instead of cars. It was all about keeping you in this consumption mode. But these visions were very captivating to me as a little kid.

"I remember when I visited the 1964 New York World's Fair," Griffith recalls, "which was one of the last naive, pre-Watergate, moving sidewalk visions of the future. The year 1964 was still kind of the fifties—the sixties hadn't really happened yet. I remember the General Electric Building presented what would be called a 'smart house.' It was the perfect house of the future, basically like walking into a robot. The whole idea was you wouldn't have to do anything. While you were at work your kitchen would be preparing the pot roast for when you got home. Parallel to that was the idea that you'd be *like* your house. You'd be in synch with this very programmed, perfect environment."

Moore notes the usual suspects to account for the failed future: Space Race burnout once America had landed men on the Moon and won Cold War bragging rights, the lack of optimism in the aftermath of the disastrous Vietnam War and the political scandals of Watergate. But back on that historic date of July 20, 1969, television images of astronauts performing their lunar tasks seemed to cinch the promised future for a thirteen-year-old Moore.

"My parents and I went to watch the Moon walk at a friend's house," Moore says. "There were all these guests gathered around the set with drinks and making toasts: 'Here's to the Man in the Moon!' I just knew this event was significant. It was a moment frozen in time. To me this showed the promise of things to come. It was like, 'Okay, we did it! Now, what's next?' It just cemented in my mind that we *were* going to have this futuristic society."

The first time man walked on the Moon, effects vet Jim Danforth was in England working on the eventual 1970 release *When Dinosaurs Ruled the Earth*. Danforth recalls that although the typical weekday broadcasting day then ended at around 10:00 P.M. television kept broadcasting so the British Isles could marvel at the transmissions from space.

"I'm grateful to have lived in these times, but the truly amazing thing to me is we went to the Moon a few times—and have never gone back!" Danforth frowns. "Now we're sending these little robots to Mars. Now, I understand it's all good science, but the big high isn't there because we as a species aren't there. Going to the Moon in 1969 was the fruition of centuries of dreams, and what has happened since is the *refutation* of those dreams. It's totally at odds with science fiction and the predictions of what would happen. We're sitting here, cocky in all our glory, and it could all end tomorrow! All it takes is one big meteorite, one little glitch in the rotation of the planet. A dust cloud goes up, the sun's rays get cut off, we plunge into cold. The Ice Age returns. Oceans wash over the world. We're too busy worrying about things like repealing a tax or surfing the Internet. It's like: 'What's on TV?'"

"It's still an amazing adventure to contemplate going back to the Moon or being in outer space," Ralph McQuarrie smiles. "I'd love to see us take a trip to Mars. There's all the possibilities of cocooning a person, slowing down their metabolism before they get to another planet. Maybe eventually we'll find a way to accelerate a body to near the speed of light. After all, at one time we didn't think we could exceed the speed of sound.

"What makes it interesting is there's no way to know what's out there. I say, drop all war, drop all the other competition, and get together in a cooperative way to discover what is out there. It's a big enough challenge to keep everybody busy for quite a long time."

The always forward-looking covers of
Science and Mechanics *predict a bracing,*
600-mph commute of the future in the streamlined
"magnetic passenger missile." (Art by Frank Tinsley.)

The Fujitsu Interactive AI paper explains why Tezuka designed a creature of the imagination:

Some imaginary beings, such as characters in Greek mythology and Japanese kappa, have indeed fascinated the human imagination for millennia because they "connect dreams and reality." Such a creature as a satyr for example—half-man, half-goat—partakes of the familiar while evoking the unknown, and thus sparks the imagination to life.

So it is with Fin Fin. He is both strange and familiar . . . And though Fin Fin hails from planet Teo, many galaxies away, he is immediately familiar to anyone who encounters him on a PC screen because he shares our emotional range.[5]

FUTURE SHOCK

Author Alvin Toffler's famous Future Shock theory (postulated in 1970) held that the evolving technologies of the near future would rapidly outstrip the capacity of humans to assimilate the traumatic consequences of accelerated change into their institutions and personal lives.

Indeed, there were a number of shocks to the system in 1997. In March, Scottish scientists created Dolly, a sheep and the first mammal cloned from adult cells—which instantly led to President Bill Clinton's proposal to ban human cloning. In 1997 researchers at Carnegie-Mellon University were also proposing the possibility of creating virtual data-

As Time *goes by, the cover imagery reflects the strange Future-Present.*

bases of an individual's entire life that would fit on a hard drive the size of a quarter. Electronic gaming companies and entire theme parks were creating ever more sophisticated simulated worlds to get lost in. Bio-computers were predicted to become incorporated into the physical body.

"Why do we know all this is coming?" a 1997 *BusinessWeek* article rhetorically asked regarding the fantastic future. "Two reasons. First, because we can bank on the same forces that unleashed the PC revolution 25 years ago: shrinking silicon circuits and faster communications infrastructure. 'The pace of change is actually accelerating now,' says Richard Howard, director of wireless research at Lucent Bell Laboratories. In the next two decades, 'we'll see explosive growth of communications, computing, memory, wireless, and broadband technology.'"[6]

Ironically, Toffler foretold that as society accelerated into a technologically driven, speeded-up future, many people would turn away from science: "One response to the loss of control . . . is a revulsion against intelligence. . . . Today, mounting evidence that society is out of control breeds disillusionment with science. In consequence, we witness a garish revival of mysticism. Suddenly astrology is the rage. . . . Cults form around the search for Dionysian experience. . . ."[7]

BRAVE NEW WORLD

"What's disturbing is that people are becoming very suspicious of science," echoes Dr. Frank Norick, an anthropologist specializing in Egyptian prehistory who retired in 1995 after nearly forty years as an assistant director and principal scientist at the University of California, Berkeley Lowie Museum of Anthropology. "Look at what's happening in genetics with the issue of cloning. You have these crazies who've never taken anything more than a high school course in genetics, if that much, who are convinced that science is going to be cloning monsters to take over the Earth. You better bet your life that scientists are going to try and clone human beings—and what's wrong with that? This is what investigation is all about. You don't set limits on what you can do. I think the urge to know is one of the most dynamic forces in the human condition.

"But we don't teach the scientific method anymore, which is to assess the evidence that you have and very deliberately arrive at whatever best explains a particular phenomenon. That's all a theory is—it's a model of explanation. That's what science is all about. But look at what happens today, with people actually making pilgrimages to see something like the stains on a garage floor that supposedly have the outline of the Virgin Mary. Reality doesn't solve problems for you, but fantasies do."

But Norick, like millions of others, was thrilled by the 1997 Pathfinder pictures transmitted from Mars and hopeful that this wonder might turn the populace away from flirtations with superstitious dogmas, conspiracy theories, and the other examples of disillusionment Toffler predicted.

"Back in the fifties *Sputnik* opened the doors in academia, caused people to want to become scientists," Norick recalls. "I was wondering about the possible effect of this Martian thing. That was really exciting! It got me to dig out this box I've saved all these years that's full of 1969 newspapers covering the Moon landing. I wonder if this latest escapade on Mars will be enough of an impetus for kids to look to science as a career."

ZIP CODE

Are we having fun yet??

—FROM THE SAYINGS OF BILL GRIFFITH'S COMIC STRIP CHARACTER ZIPPY THE PINHEAD

Perhaps it was his youth growing up in the prototypical post–World War II housing tract development of Levittown (which has been called the origin of modern suburbia) that gave Bill Griffith his skewed take on not only the usual mortal foibles but also the modern world's monolithic scale, particularly the vagaries of pop culture and the intoxicating power of mass media. Griffith's vehicle is the comic strip incarnation of a microcephalic, or "pinhead," a figure traditionally associated with the old carny freak shows of the past. Zippy was born in 1970 in the pages of the underground comix magazine *Real Pulp*. Somehow Zippy got a daily syndicated comic strip gig under the banner of the venerable King Features Syndicate. The strip also features Zip's sidekick Griffy, a character who faces the modern world perpetually aghast.

Griffith, who holds sway over what he calls a "tiny, but highly influential, cult following," has explained that his function as writer and artist is to let Zippy out of his psyche, listen to Zippy's insights, translate it all into each strip—and then deny all responsibility. "Zippy is a way out of the stress and tension of always having to deal with what we all decide is real," Griffith explains. "To Zippy that's always up for grabs." Or as Zippy himself has put it: "Reality is a sandwich I did not order."

As a jumping-off point for a mental romp from the sixties to the nineties, Griffith laughingly recalls showing up at the Human Be-in held at San Francisco's Golden Gate Park, that ultimate 1967 "Summer of Love" epochal hippie event, dressed in a shiny blue suit and wearing cordovan wing tips. . . .

"I went to the Be-in determined to be an observer and not be mistaken for a participant. The Group Mind always scares me, and that event was primarily about letting go of your ego and being part of the group. I was always skeptical of the hippie movement. There was such pressure to be a certain way. That kind of thinking makes me think of people with boots and armbands marching through the streets and smashing windows.

"When I started Zippy he was a very surrealistic character who was defined by a non sequitur speech pattern that was like a TV set with the dial changing constantly. The character was something of a metaphor for the information overload of 1970, which was like thirteen channels and some newspapers and magazines. Now, in 1997, we've got television with *hundreds of channels*, the Internet, just thousands more times the bombardment of information. It shows how incredibly malleable the human mind is that after all these years our brains haven't just exploded. It's almost like we're in the process of reprogramming our genetic alterations to accommodate this onrush of information.

"We're also definitely being taught by the media to embrace the techno-future and always have been. Technology has become America's religion. To me Microsoft CEO Bill Gates is like the director of this, the man-behind-the-curtain of the future of techno-America. It's really revenge of the nerds, with Bill Gates at the top of the pyramid down to the computer hackers and kids obsessed with video games and addicted to the Internet. Gates's whole idea is WebTV [an actual Silicon Valley startup purchased by Gates], in which all your practical needs will be connected through your TV screen: entertainment, shopping, banking, voting, Web access. To me it's a very grim future, a controlled environment for the sake of corporate needs, not human needs.

"One thread that's really developed since the fifties and the first Disneyland was built, is that today a huge percentage of Americans actually take their vacations at theme parks. But it makes perfect sense. A theme park is where you go where nothing surprising happens. Everything is scripted, and even the surprises are all programmed and you know when they're coming. You're acting your role, the way people act their roles in daily life. Maybe that's the future in many ways.

"In Las Vegas there's now this Disneyland aspect; it's become a kind of adult amusement park. Of course, it's gambling that brings people there, but Vegas is now being promoted as this wholesome place for Americans to live and visit. Vegas is the biggest-growing population center of the United States! I think Vegas took over from L.A. as some kind of vision of hope for Americans, which is really twisted. L.A. at least had orange groves and this glowing Pacific Ocean visual appeal to people in the twenties and thirties. But Las Vegas to me represents greed, danger, and the dark side of America. And maybe *that's* the appeal.

"We're definitely a more cynical culture now and everyone points to Watergate as the watershed where all the illusions we had about our government and the authority figures in our lives came crashing down. That was an unveiling moment. The emperor has no clothes.

"We don't actually even believe in commercials anymore. Commercials used to have to create artificial needs. But people are too cynical to fall for a sales pitch. You look at commercials now and they instead sell an image or attitude that goes with the product. You're not buying a car, you're buying an attitude toward freedom or something. Commercials tell stories now. You experience them, and the product is almost subliminal. Then you pick up the product later because it's been implanted in your brain.

"As a culture we don't feel the connection between the present and the past. Everything is present. You have entire TV stations devoted to rerunning TV shows from the fifties, sixties, and seventies, which takes them out of the context of the times in which they were made and makes them into these kind of kitsch objects. The context in which they existed doesn't resonate anymore. A kid today watching a program from the sixties has no reference point to understand when these shows were made, so they become a silly parade of old values and attitudes, something to laugh at. I even remember people of my generation, back in the midsixties and later, watching old Humphrey Bogart films in repertory theaters and laughing at them! The values seemed so out of date, or we wanted to feel superior to them. But this has been going on ever since we started recycling our culture.

"The really frightening thing is we're now parodying and recycling things from an ever-closer moment in history. Pretty soon we're going to say things like, 'Remember July? July was hysterical, wasn't it?' Or, 'Remember last week? Man, that was funny.' It's just getting so close. I don't know what'll happen when we can't cannibalize the past anymore because it's all been cannibalized right up till yesterday. We're eventually going to reach that point. I don't know what happens then.

"But I've always had a love/hate relationship with American culture in general, popular culture especially. At its best it's kind of a beautiful

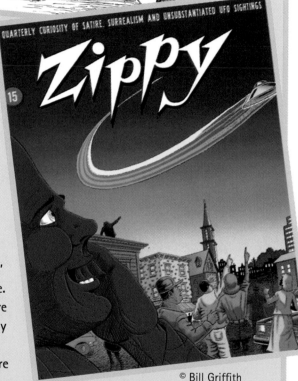

© Bill Griffith

thing. Because of what I do I've had some Hollywood experiences that to me have always involved a kind of playground quality. Things like staying at the Chateau Marmont [a famous Hollywood hotel], these places that kind of exist in a fantastical way and seeing them in their real state brings you into that fantasy.

"I recently went to this new restaurant in San Francisco and we were put in the best seat in the place, which was this corner booth. And the waitress came over and she wanted us to be sure we realized that I was sitting in the *very spot* where Sharon Stone had been sitting the night before. So, my butt was immediately tingling with celebrity delight. It was like saying some god sat here! The waitress wanted us to know we were on hallowed ground."

The menacing Robot controlled by Dr. Smith is unveiled for New Line's feature film take on the Lost in Space *saga.*

THE VIRTUAL REALM

In the view of many people . . . the time is upon us when the computer will be able to take on graphic tasks . . . including the simulation of reality. All that is needed for realistic scene simulation, in fact, is a computer that devours numbers the way a whale devours plankton and software capable of conveying to that computer what, for example, a suburban garden looks like at six P.M. on a spring evening.

—CHRISTOPHER FINCH, SPECIAL EFFECTS: CREATING MOVIE MAGIC, 1984

There was a time, not too long ago, when it was a fantastical notion to imagine a computer capable of creating a perfectly photorealistic image, particularly of organic natural phenomena.

Certainly it was unheard of in the era of the *Lost in Space* TV show, a time of traditional physical effects ranging from "in-camera" tricks and models flown on wires to alien landscapes conjured up on stage with painted vista and sky backings. Even the high-end effects production of the sixties—director Stanley Kubrick's 1968 feature *2001: A Space Odyssey*—pushed the envelope in some effects areas (such as the streak photography "slit-scan" required for the famed Stargate Corridor light show sequence), but still resorted to such classic illusions as miniature models and in-camera multiple exposures. *2001* even conveyed the weightlessness of space by flying actors on wires, the same gag George Pal had used eighteen years earlier on *Destination Moon*.

The first high-resolution examples of computer-generated imagery were simple wireframe constructs, but by 1997 computer-generated and image-processed imagery is both photorealistic and omnipresent—from movies and television to electronic games and virtual-reality theme parks. The *Lost in Space* movie has benefited from the new digital tool kit, with three-dimensional computer-generated spacecraft replacing the model ships of old. Now alien environments and creatures can be conjured up without the physical and photochemical constraints of traditional effects.

THE DIGITAL ADVANTAGE

It's a complex process to create a three-dimensional character or object. In the high-end, high-resolution medium of movies an absolute must are high-powered computer hardware systems to crunch the numbers and process incredible amounts of information. (All computer data is stored as a binary digit, a numbering system based on the digits 1 and 0). To create high-end, high-resolution three-dimensional images often requires special noncommercial software programs. Ultimately the final image depends on the talent of the artist, not merely the sophistication of the tools.

One of the major advantages of working in the limitless realm of cyberspace is the "virtual camera," with which a CG artist can essentially

(OPPOSITE TOP AND BOTTOM) *Matt LeBlanc and additional performer in front of green screens. Both green and blue screens are used to film performers for effects shots. Once scanned into a computer the photographed "element" can be extracted from the neutral colored screen background and digitally composited into whatever background is desired—whether a separately shot live action environment or a completely synthetic, computer-generated one.* (ABOVE) *The new* Jupiter 2 *suspended animation chambers.* (RIGHT) *All hell breaks loose on the* Jupiter 2.

The Lost in Space Jupiter 2 *command deck.*

"film" a scene in the computer without the hindrances or even potential physical dangers that a flesh-and-blood cinematographer might face. The virtual camera, in fact, defies physical laws—it can fly through the air at super speeds, turn on a dime, even go *through* objects if need be.

One of the major effects breakthroughs came in the 1977 release of *Star Wars*, with creator/director George Lucas and his production crew ushering in the era of "motion control," a computerized system by which cameras, props, and models could be programmed to move in repeatable ways. This breakthrough allowed for separately filmed elements to be composited into complex, multi-image visions using an "optical printer" (a Machine Age device in which those separately filmed elements are individually projected into the eye of a rolling camera loaded with fresh film).

The resulting success of the *Star Wars* trilogy also provided Lucas the development capital with which his Lucasfilm company began to stretch the technological envelope. Lucas's ultimate dream was to replace the old photochemical optical printers with an electronic input/output scanner that could convert film into digital information for compositing and processing and then be output to film (with the completed effects shot then able to be cut in with the rest of the film). But Lucasfilm was also

leading the way on some of the earliest high-resolution experiments into totally synthetic 3-D imagery.

The first all-CG scene ever put into a feature film was the "Genesis Sequence" in 1982's *Star Trek II: The Wrath of Khan*. The sequence, produced by Lucasfilm's Computer Division, showed a device being shot through space onto a lifeless world that ignited a pillar of fire that spread across the barren landscape, leaving a verdant paradise in its wake. Many of the creative leaders of that pioneering Lucasfilm Computer Division would eventually leave to form Pixar, which produced 1995's breakthrough all-CG film *Toy Story*. Meanwhile, Industrial Light & Magic had gone on to perfect Lucas's dream of that digital input/output system, as well as to create such 3-D breakthroughs as the seemingly flesh-and-blood dinosaurs of 1993's *Jurassic Park*.

Merrill Dean, our ham radio buddy, recalls having a business lunch with George Lucas in 1978 and remembers how prescient Lucas was about the way in which emerging technologies would someday transform every aspect of moviemaking. "George and I were talking about the future of motion picture distribution. He said that one day, instead of making all the prints for a theatrical release, a producer would have one print put up digitally via satellite and there'd be a high-definition television transmission simultaneously to exhibitors around the world—producers would make all their money back in one day. You'd have a worldwide marketing campaign, everybody would be in the theaters at the same time, and all the exhibitors would just pull the signal down from a satellite. Digital signals? Who back then was even thinking of describing a picture digitally as opposed to an analog version with cathode tubes and all that? And now, in 1997, it's just starting to happen, with digital TV and all the cable systems gearing up for digital delivery of signals."

ART OF THE COMPUTER

In one episode of *Lost in Space*, Will is seen working an old-fashioned mainframe computer requiring punched cards. Such was the technological reality of the midsixties, a time when computer scientists were generally cloistered in academic sanctums, developing the technology to serve the needs of government, science, and industry. But in 1964 an art professor at Ohio State University named Charles Csuri began to use the technology for a radical purpose—art.

Nowadays the computer has become an indispensable tool in commercial art, with software able to replicate the grainy and gritty textures of traditional oil and brush painting. But while popular commercial "paint" programs, such as Adobe's Photoshop, allow for the manipulation of images, Csuri still writes, or has written for him, proprietary programs that help him achieve his unique artistic visions. "Today I'm tied to a network where I have access to computers that have five times the firepower that I use on my own computer," Csuri explains. "I'm in an environment [at Ohio State University] where there is technical support with people developing software."

In the early to midsixties Csuri was friends with the likes of the late Roy Lichtenstein, one of the founders of the Pop Art movement (which reflected the ephemeral popular mediums, such as comic books and advertising icons, within such traditional arts as painting and sculpture). Csuri was tempted to become part of that New York art scene, but decided instead to remain at Ohio State University. Part of the reason was his anathema for the politics of the art world. But the most compelling reason was that in 1964 he'd seen an image of a woman's face in profile that had been generated on a printer. The implication "hit me like a bolt of lightning," Csuri told *Smithsonian* magazine.[1]

The image had instantly coalesced a long gestation period during which he had been contemplating the mysteries and artistic potential of the computer. "Back in 1955 a friend of mine who was an industrial engineer told me he was working on a computer and I asked, 'What's a computer?'" Csuri recalls in his soft-spoken voice. "I went through the stage of asking what a computer program was, what an algorithm was. This was before there were any display devices that could make an image, way before computer graphics. I was thinking in terms of transformations and I was absorbing information about digital computers without realizing it. In 1963, with my friend's advice, I built a mechanical-type drawing machine based upon the principle of a pantograph. I was able to make transformations on my drawings, a process that's now called analogue computer art."

Csuri's computer art, which he exhibits as still images on paper, ranges from exploring colors as emanations

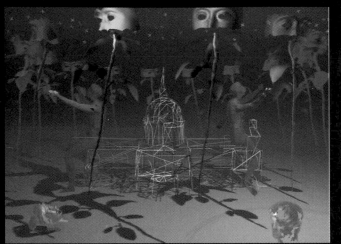

In Search of Meaning

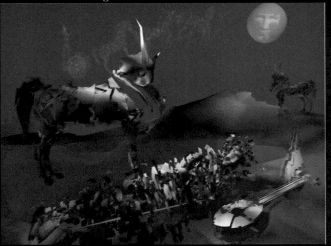

Sleeping Gypsy

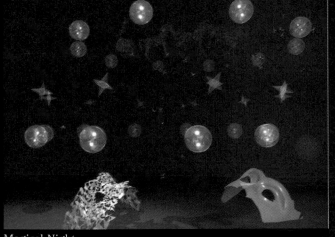

Magical Night

of light to pieces inspired by classical art itself (such as the fifteenth-century Masaccio fresco *The Expulsion from Paradise*, reflected in Csuri's *Phases of Morning*). Other artwork shows images unraveling, shattering into fragments.

One of his earliest images, produced on a four-by-six-foot length of paper, depicted a battlefield filled with figures of red and black toy soldiers. "I had hundreds of these soldiers from my database and each side would have its wounded, the dead, even the Medal of Honor winners," Csuri says. "Then I took the names of my colleagues in the art department and the administrators of the university and entered their names in a computer program that generated a random number determining who got killed, wounded, or was the Medal of Honor winner. And above the scene was a sheet of paper printing the names of the people that were identified with the particular soldiers in this environment. It personalized the nature of war. And that became the art object."

Csuri has seen the technology evolve from early vector graphics (which programmed coordinates to connect dot-to-dot to create line drawings) to raster graphics (which graduated the medium to images made up of tiny picture element dots, or "pixels"). He himself has graduated from the earliest mainframe and coded-card-driven stylus (which didn't even allow for a monitor to watch the works in progress) to his nineties hardware: a Silicon Graphics Indigo 2 with some eight gigabytes of disc space and 128 megabytes of memory. Vital to his presentation is special paper upon which he prints his final computer-generated images.

"The art object to me is not the color image you see on the computer monitor, because everybody's monitor has a different color quality," Csuri notes. "The final art objects I produce are still images produced on acid-free paper with an ink-jet printer. There's an outfit in New York that's helping me with an acid-free, textured paper that's made a tremendous difference in my imagery, in the way they are presented and perceived. If you would see them in a gallery, and nobody told you how they were done, you wouldn't think computer. They look like fine art prints."

Csuri has also gotten involved with other emerging technologies. At the 1997 Siggraph Conference in Los Angeles, Csuri was on hand to demonstrate art pieces he'd created using new 3-D technology developed by Dimensional Media Associates of New York. "The device is called an auto stereoscopic display," Csuri notes, "for three-dimensional animation. When played and viewed, an image looks as if it were floating in space with the feeling of a hologram. The device uses a background video system, the background monitor, then a foreground projection system. What is remarkable is you don't need to wear special goggles [as in normal 3-D movie presentations].

"It's still not what we all keep hoping for, which is a life-size holographic display system which can produce, say, what looks like a moving person but which is in fact a synthetic image. You could have a figure dancing in front of you, even entire theatrical performances—all synthetic creations. In the process of doing it and thinking about it I found myself starting to think about 3-D sculptures, about a different art form, although it's premature to call this an art form. If your object hits the edge of the screen, the three-dimensional quality collapses, it simply converts back into an ordinary video. Since it limited my range of motion, I had to keep the objects very simple."

Csuri's "simple" objects for the new 3-D technology ranged from his "motion sculpture" of an ancient ruined classical Greek head sculpture, complete with butterflies flapping in and out and around the head (which itself rotated clockwise and counterclockwise in continuous motion), to an image of the ancient Egyptian queen Nefertiti balancing on the edge of a giant flying paper airplane.

But while Csuri is intrigued with the possibilities of holographic technology, the year 1997 saw him going down a new path. His real dream is to create what he calls "cognitive art objects," basically entire 3-D environments in which computer-generated art objects can take on a life of their own, arranging themselves into a final composition selected by the artist.

Csuri's beginnings didn't fit the mold of the computer nerd: At Ohio State he was not only majoring in painting but starring on the football field. As a six-foot, 210-pound tackle, he led his football team to the national championship in his junior year and was honored with an All-American selection. His college coach, the great Paul Brown, would go on to the pros and eventually invite Csuri to join him. However, Csuri's senior year was interrupted by World War II and a three-year hitch in the army (including being at the Battle of the Bulge), which changed his life . . .

"The thing about being in combat is it does affect you when you're on a battlefield and you see body parts lying around. You see the misery that comes from human beings destroying one another. You end up having a different perspective about a great many things. My war experiences did make a difference in terms of

Introspection

Ribbon Romp

my decision to get a graduate degree at Ohio State and not play with the Cleveland Browns when my old college coach Paul Brown invited me to play professional football. I simply did not want to hit anybody or have anybody hit me.

"I was exhibiting paintings in New York and Roy [Lichtenstein] was introducing me to all the people in the Pop Art movement. I got a sense of how things worked in the art world and I decided to stay at Ohio State University. Shortly thereafter is when I discovered the computer. There was an excitement during that period about concepts of artificial intelligence and different forms of media. In fact, I may well be the first professional artist to get involved with the computer.

"My first computer images might have been line drawings of a housefly or a hummingbird. The first computer artwork I did was printed out on computer paper. In the late sixties I did what I called a 'real-time art object,' an illusion of three-dimensional butterflies flying in real time, flapping their wings and moving around, and I had the ability to control them interactively.

"In the beginning you'd write a computer program and then the large IBM mainframe computer would give you back a stack of cards which coded your program. You'd stack the cards into a kind of carriage on a 'drum plotter,' which was basically another small computer. It would read each card and send this information to the smaller computer, which would make an ink-and-pen drawing for you, driving the stylus, a penlike device, across paper mounted on a drum. What was happening internally is the computer program took that data and it recognized where that stylus was going and it recalculated and repositioned the object. This went on for three or four years and then I got involved with a vector display, that line-drawing beam, and that's when I got really excited by real-time art objects.

"About 1968 I received my first National Science Foundation grant. I got intrigued with basic research and spent the next twenty-two years working on basic research in computer graphics, helping develop the field. It gave me insight into how technology works and helped me to understand what I could do as an artist. I believe what happens with technology is you eventually adjust and work within its constraints. Certainly there are all kinds of frustrations about trying to have control over the medium while you have aspirations to do more complex things.

"My approach is not to use a Mac paint system like Photoshop. For what I do you have to know computer programming. I have to think in terms of how things will be positioned in space, their surface properties, lighting and light sources, what are the colors and shadows. I have to write programs that enable me to do these things procedurally, to set up rules.

"When I first started working with computers I had the attitude of a traditional artist in the way that I looked at color and space, the way that I set up an environment to create an image. But as I understood the technological tools and its implications, what it meant to do procedural programming, I found myself looking at creativity from a different point of view. I try to set up conditions where the creative process is more a process of discovery. I try to exploit the kinds of things that computers can do and what the technology can offer. I've moved away from thinking like a traditional artist.

"I think the sort of thing I'm moving toward now is using the computer to create environments and situations that I think of as cognitive art objects. Let me explain. Ordinarily in computer graphics when people think of a three-dimensional object they think of its geometry, its color, its surface properties, and so on. Usually that's as far as it goes. What I'm thinking of now is objects that have certain behaviors, kinetic structures, even sounds identified with them. Most important, they will have a capability to do message passing between them. The objects will be able to communicate with one another. For instance, [asking each other]: 'What is your size?' 'Do not bump into me.' 'Can we compromise about color and size?' 'How many copies of myself?' 'No, this time I'm using my own light source and atmosphere.' 'What level of abstraction do you want me to be?'

"Let's say I've defined an object in the scene as being Picasso. And any of the figures or objects who get near Picasso have to shrink in size or have to bow and pay homage to Picasso. So I'm the Supreme Advisor and I set up the rules and constraints about how the objects can relate to one another, although I give them some latitude. There is a loop and the objects make decisions. The idea is that at five o'clock, when I go home, I start this game and overnight the objects on their own go through maybe one hundred versions of a scene. When I return I'll look at low-resolution pictures of each and I might decide that Number Twenty-five has real possibilities. Maybe change this or that and you have a final work of art. I'm trying to think of the computer as a process of discovery, where I create an environment that basically does a search for me.

The Past Casts Shadows

Garden Lovers

"I'm talking, in a sense, about the future, of where I think art is going. In terms of three dimensions, you have so many more complex variables to deal with. The kind of software development I'm talking about is on its way. The commercial world hasn't quite reached this stage yet, but I think once they do they'll leap all over it because there'll be money to be made. Even doing special effects in films has become so complex that I think people will be taking a fresh look at how to create scenes and software development.

"One of the things I never expected when I started out was how big computer graphics would become in the film industry. About twenty to twenty-five years ago, Frank Thomas and Ollie Johnston [famed Disney animators] came to see me here in Columbus, Ohio, because we were doing things in computer animation that nobody else was doing on either coast and they were very excited by it. Of course, a whole gang of my former students have gone out into the film industry, which is really nice.

"Thinking back to the midsixties, all of this was unknown. It's very hard for people today to imagine the most primitive things at the beginning. It was so hard to figure out how to do simple lighting effects with a computer or to create a computer language that would allow you to control objects moving through space. Today it's no big deal—any ten-year-old can do it! But it's different at the outset, when a field has not been defined, when it's really and truly new territory. But I must admit that while it was really difficult at the beginning, it was exciting to be able to do something that had never been done before. That's been very gratifying."

Lost in Space

THE ABC SATURDAY SUPERSTAR MOVIE

The classic Lost in Space *TV show was celebrated in such ancillary forms as bubble gum cards, board games, lunch boxes—and a Saturday morning "superstar movie."*

⊕ POP '97

CHICAGO—From the bleachers of Wrigley Field to the plush seats of the Lyric Opera, Chicago has long been a center of real entertainment with real performers. . . . But with Walt Disney Co. and Steven Spielberg dreaming up huge "virtual reality theme parks" for Chicago, the City that Works stands on the brink of becoming a national center for high-tech fantasies—the City that Zaps, Levitates, Escapes and, promoters hope, Spends.

—STEVE KLOEHN AND FLYNN MCROBERTS, FEATURE ARTICLE IN THE CHICAGO TRIBUNE, AUGUST 19, 1997

The above *Chicago Tribune* item detailed the projected 1999 unveiling of DisneyQuest, a 90,000-square-foot "computerized family playland" (with a similar Disney "cyberpark" opening in Orlando, Florida) and the plans of Steven Spielberg's GameWorks to open a 30,000-square-foot virtual reality arcade and upscale nightclub/eatery (joining similar GameWorks ventures in such places as Seattle and Las Vegas). According to the *Tribune* piece, "the scale and the ability to immerse the consumer in virtual reality" are what set this new generation of theme parks apart from the typical electronic diversions of a video arcade.[1]

Welcome to 1997, when one can be immersed in simulations of reality—or fantasies made real.

The Third Eye culture of old had its own relative scale and merchandising tie-ins. The *Lost in Space* TV show, for example, had its own spin-offs: Topps bubble gum trading cards, school lunch boxes, model kits, and board games. But today's pop culture has become big business—the aforementioned DisneyQuest game centers alone are estimated to be a decade-long, *$1 billion* venture.

These days, when a particular medium brings forth a new creation, that character's image and aesthetic will be replicated through, and translated for, many other mediums and ancillary merchandising. Comic book characters such as Batman and Superman transcend the two-dimensional borders of the printed comic page and become the stuff of film and television programming, theme park rides, electronic games, toy action figures, books and games, clothing lines, video and laser disc releases—there's probably a lunch box tie-in there as well.

The rule of the jungle for Pop Culture '97 is if you stand still, *you die*. Even Superman, the 1938 archetype from which sprung the American superhero genre, underwent a startling makeover in 1997, with the iconic costumed figure of old transformed into a capeless figure wearing a white and blue outfit, the distinctive "S" chest logo refashioned into a jagged, lightning-bolt-like slash consistent with what DC Comics publishers have called Superman's newfangled "energy-based" powers.

One of the more successful recent pop creations that's wired itself into the new multimedia pop zeitgeist is the occult-edged comic book superhero *Spawn*.

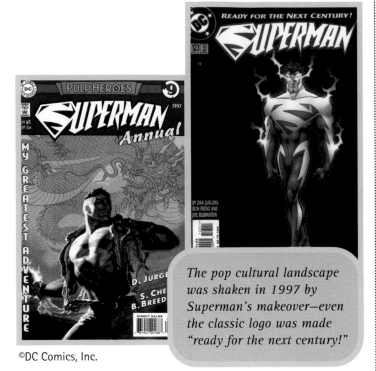

©DC Comics, Inc.

The pop cultural landscape was shaken in 1997 by Superman's makeover—even the classic logo was made "ready for the next century!"

SPAWN

Todd McFarlane, creator of *Spawn*, is a comic book writer/artist who represents the new breed of comics creator. The new generation demands total control, unlike the artist-for-hire days, when comic book publishers owned the rights and controlled the commercial destiny of the ideas and characters produced by creators in their employ. McFarlane, for example, had been making a fine living scripting and drawing Marvel Comics' star character *Spider-Man* (earning, by his own estimates, between $1 and $2 million annually). Then McFarlane and a group of fellow Marvel creators left the comics industry leader to start up Image, their own comics publishing company.

Spawn was launched as an Image title in 1992, and the first issue broke all expectations by selling an estimated 1.7 million copies. In the ensuing five years, the continuing series has sold more than 80 million copies worldwide. *Spawn* commercial tie-ins are developed and controlled through Todd McFarlane Productions—a toy line alone has generated $23 million annually. In 1997 *Spawn* was unleashed in both an animated HBO series and a summer New Line fea-

ture film release. But despite such high-powered enterprises, McFarlane says he's not driven by lawyers and marketing surveys. "When I created *Spawn* I just did it," he shrugs. "I've gone with a gut feeling. My guess is as good as anybody's market plan."

McFarlane's character is a dead man, a government assassin named Al Simmons who has been killed and literally makes a deal with the devil to be able to reunite with his beloved wife. But Simmons not only discovers that his wife is happily remarried to his best friend, but that his own face and form have been hideously scarred. His sorry consolation is the gift of superpowers. His masked form features a fantastic flapping cape that seems to have a life of its own and a uniform festooned with spikes, chains, and skulls. It's the spirit and look of the new breed of hero: amoral and violent, lost in apocalyptic landscapes and crime-ridden war zones.

McFarlane, a native of Canada, was born in 1961, the same year the Marvel comics team of writer Stan Lee and artist Jack Kirby unleashed the *Fantastic Four*. In its day, the *FF* were revolutionary, themselves an evolutionary leap over the traditional square-jawed, heart-of-gold superhero. The *FF*, as well as *Spider-Man* and the rest of the Marvel line-up, were superpowered characters with *problems*. Helping bring these more three-dimensional characters to life was the powerful art of the late Kirby, a comics veteran who had drawn propaganda icon *Captain America* during the forties.

"Jack Kirby was about energy," McFarlane says. "Jack influenced my style because he had a sense of power, a KA-POW, that left you with a couple of moments when you finished the comic book. Back in the midsixties comics characters had energy and pizzazz. You could also only get away with so much. The definition now is more of a big, gun-toting guy kicking down doors. But the vast majority of characters still aren't that way. It's no different from a video store where you've got everything from PG-13 to X-rated material. In the sixties

Todd McFarlane's Spawn *gave birth to a veritable cottage industry, beginning with the character's debut in 1992* (TOP LEFT). *(Cover art by Todd McFarlane. Spawn #1, May 1992, an Image Comics title published by Malibu Comics.) Despite Spawn's classic superhero stance* (ABOVE) *the character will remember his death and a pact made with the forces of Hell itself* (LEFT). *(Both images from Spawn #1, pages 8–9, 20.)* ™ *and* ©Todd McFarlane Productions, Inc.

the main comics demographics was ages seven to thirteen; now it's twelve to twenty-five. But what I loved as a kid is not that much different from what kids love today: aliens, dinosaurs, monsters.

"There's a theology in *Spawn*, but it's still about good and evil. My character might be edgy, but you can't just create another Superman. *Spawn* made the adjustment, although some people might not get it because they're used to a Boy Scout. Comics have advanced and evolved like everything else in society. For example, you couldn't just gear the *Lost in Space* movie to the generation that remembers the black-and-white season of the TV show. You have to re-create that world, modernize it so it can compete."

McFarlane has Spawn's destiny mapped out, a future path that will forge ahead until his character becomes so big that other writers and artists can pick up and perpetuate the saga far into the future. "I know the ending, I know where Spawn is evolving," he says mysteriously. "I haven't abandoned my baby. He's only five years old. I can raise the kid, see him to graduate school, raise him so he can go out in the world. I'm open to the character continuing.

"My goal when I started *Spawn* was to create my own icon, raise him until he becomes bigger than me. Walt Disney is gone, but his character Mickey Mouse lives on. Can I create the same thing? Can I have this character who will still be around on this planet after I'm gone?"

THE GAME FACE

The pop culture is also wired into electronic games, whether hand-held devices, computer CD-ROM media, or games played off of television screens. These interactive games offer a contrast of technology, if not sensibility, compared to the sixties.

Consider this 1963 comic book advertisement for a board game:

The Complete Space Game: BLAST OFF

Adventure through our entire solar system, thrill as you try to conquest [sic] each strange planet. Establish your engineer and military quarters, raise your flag signifying possession, erect your launch pad and then BLAST OFF to your next space conquest.

In contrast, consider this 1997 comic book ad describing the modern electronic incarnation of a Blast Off board game:

*BUILD IT, PROGRAM IT, UNLEASH IT:
CARNAGE HEART*

Jupiter, 2073. Not a place for the faint-of-heart. Nor the weak-of-mind. Mechanized armies run amok, and you must develop the strategies and alliances to quell the chaos. Go from blueprint to battlefield as you design, build, program and launch your mechanized warriors into conflict in the first in-depth strategy game for your playstation game console.

For the modern, media-hyped kid, the new breed of game allows one to control technology and become immersed in a virtual experience. There's *Sim Earth: The Living Planet*, designed for play on the Super Nintendo Entertainment System, which boasts: "You've got the whole world in your hands!" In the game, a player can be master of one of eight planets, or simply create a new world and the ecology and life forms on it, even control the evolution of species and "experiment with global warming and nuclear war."

As a 1993 *Sim Earth* comic book ad notes:

"Play SimEarth and create new worlds and civilizations . . . then watch over them for a few billion years! There's never been another world like the one you build . . . Move mountains, destroy continents. Watch the results of volcanos, earthquakes and tidal waves. Each and every second you'll be making decisions that will have incredible repercussions billions of years into the future!"

THE FARAWAY GALAXY

One of the most unusual award presentations in history was the moment during the 1992 Academy Awards ceremony when George Lucas stepped onto the stage to accept the Irving G. Thalberg Award. Lucas's friend and colleague Steven Spielberg presented the award with the words: "Like his creation Luke Skywalker, George Lucas continues to look into the future and dream."

Then the stage curtains parted and upon a giant screen flashed an image from space—the crew of the space shuttle *Atlantis*. Flight commander Charlie Bolden read the taped message: "The imagination and ingenuity that have turned dreams into the reality of space flight are no different than those which turn ideas and inspirations into motion pictures."

That moment—a fusion of the dream of outer space and the reality of space exploration—was also a celebration of the impact of *Star Wars* on the culture. "*Star Wars* made space fun, but its appeal is rooted in the journey that everybody has to take," says Lucasfilm producer Rick McCallum.

One of the major pop culture events of 1997 was the twentieth-anniversary theatrical rerelease of the *Star Wars* trilogy. The so-called "Special Editions" shattered all box office expectations, generating more than $250 million in the U.S. alone. For the occasion, Lucas's ILM division had even integrated into the original footage new, computer-generated effects sequences and digitally processed out any telltale "matte lines" (the black outlines around traditionally photochemically composited elements), with Lucasfilm and Twentieth Century Fox also heading up a major restoration effort on *Star Wars* in particular.

The year 1997 also saw production commence on the next chapters in the *Star Wars* saga—the so-called prequels, which will pick up the storyline in the time of the young Anakin Skywalker (whom audiences know as the adult Darth Vader). To prequel producer Rick McCallum, eight-year-old Anakin actor Jake Lloyd has the spirit of modern youth that is unafraid to look up at the stars and dream.

"There's no question in Jake's mind that there's other people out there," McCallum says. "George [Lucas] and I were talking to him and it was obvious he was not only obsessed by this notion, but that he categorically knows there are other people out in the universe. He just knows. He's a special kid. He has an enormous faith in life. He believes anything is possible."

McCallum, whose Lucasfilm career has also included producing *The Young Indiana Jones* TV series, has described as "one of the greatest aspects of the job" the opportunity to conjure up a different time period—even an entire alien world—and inhabit it for the duration of a production. "During *Young Indy* I've lived in the world of 1908, 1918, and 1939," McCallum says. "Then, when I was working on the *Star Wars Trilogy Special Edition,* I spent two and a half years in the most bizarre world, a world that was twenty years ago, but represents a world millions of years ago. And now, with the prequels, I'm in a world that's a little older, one I originally experienced when I was twenty-three and saw *Star Wars* for the first time."

During 1997 the Lucasfilm prequel production went back to the deserts of Tunisia—where Luke Skywalker's home planet of Tatooine was originally created for *Star Wars*—to build a new village, a new vision of Tatooine. "We were in a different site in Tunisia from the original *Star Wars*," McCallum notes, "but I swear that within a couple weeks of our being there—we were on Tatooine! We not only made Tatooine, we got to *be* there. We made our own world. There were those [on the production] who had to have their comforts, but for us adventurous types it felt like we were on another planet."

⑪ MESSAGES FROM SPACE

> *We shall not cease from exploration*
> *And the end of all our exploring*
> *Will be to arrive where we started*
> *And know the place for the first time.*
>
> **—T. S. ELIOT, FOUR QUARTETS**

t was the Christmas season of 1968 when "man broke his bonds to Earth," as NASA put it. For the first time human beings had rocketed free from Earth's gravity, sending *Apollo 8* astronauts James Lovell Jr., Frank Borman, and William Anders on the first manned orbit around the Moon. On Christmas Day the spacecraft completed its tenth and final orbit, swung into a transearth course, and headed for home.

The three astronauts were also the first humans to see planet Earth whole from deep space. "The vast loneliness up here is awe-inspiring, and it makes you realize just what you have back there on Earth," Lovell remarked from space. "The Earth from here is a grand oasis. . . . Waters are all sort of a royal blue, clouds of course are bright white."[1]

It would be at Christmastime, four years later, that *Apollo 17* would return from the Moon—marking the last earthly visitation to that barren world. The space program by 1997 had long since shifted from manned extraterrestrial voyages to unmanned deep space probes and shuttle and space station missions above Earth's atmosphere.

SPACE EPIPHANY

For the twelve astronauts who have walked on the Moon, the experience was life-changing. *Apollo 15* astronaut Jim Irwin talked of the beauty of the Moon mountains and "felt the presence of God."

"I remember on the trip home on *Apollo 11* it suddenly struck me that that tiny pea, pretty and blue, was the Earth," Neil Armstrong recalled. "I put up my thumb and shut one eye, and my thumb blotted out the planet Earth. I didn't feel like a giant. I felt very, very small."[2]

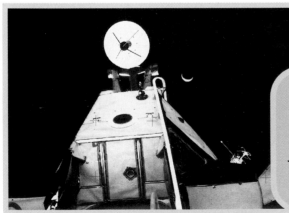

Close-up view of forward section of the Apollo 14 *lunar module on the Moon. While lunar module pilot Edgar Mitchell and mission commander Alan Shepard (who also helped pioneer the era of space exploration as the first American into space), went about their extravehicular activities (EVA), Stuart Roosa kept the Command and Services Modules in lunar orbit.*

"Something happens to you out there," *Apollo 14* astronaut Edgar Mitchell, the sixth man to walk on the Moon, told *Time* magazine a year after his own extraterrestrial voyage.[3]

While many of the Moon walkers have described their experience in spiritual terms, Mitchell has arguably made the most significant voyages into the vastness of internal space, into the very nature of consciousness.

Mitchell fit the classic fifties image of the superman astronaut. Born into a cattle-ranching family, he spent most of his formative years in Roswell, New Mexico, inculcating what he has called the "mythic values of the Old West." He graduated from MIT in aeronautics and astronautics, was a naval jet aircraft pilot who flew missions during the Korean War era, and ultimately piloted the *Apollo 14* lunar module to the surface of the Moon.

One wouldn't assume, from such a background, that this paragon of the "Right Stuff" astronaut would also be conducting surreptitious extrasensory perception experiments with earthbound subjects while on his *Apollo* mission. The results intrigued him enough to found in 1972 the Institute of Noetic Sciences, a nonprofit organization dedicated to the study of all forms of human potential, particularly aspects of paranormal phenomena. Whether with the Institute or on his own, Mitchell has spent the past quarter-century seeking to unlock the secret of consciousness itself—and in 1997 he believed he'd come up with a model to explain the nature of the universe itself.

In retrospect, Mitchell had always felt the tug of the material and mystical worlds. In his book *The Way of the Explorer*, Mitchell describes the early intuitive feelings that drew him into the realm of flight.

From the very beginning I was drawn to the cutting edge of flight technology as though by some mysterious force. And I was welcomed there. . . . There was a special sense in flying, as though the aircraft were an extension of my body, which made me stand out as a pilot. It lent me the perception that there was some larger purpose that I was fulfilling. . . .

As I look back on it now, the country seemed young and new then, with the advent of nuclear technology, the jet engine, and rocketry. . . . Spaceflight was still only the dream of a handful of scientists. But when I did that first navy jet, I knew this was where I was supposed to be.[4]

Mitchell recalls how during the Korean War he was flying a P2V on a routine night patrol near the city of Shanghai. The radar operator on his aircraft spotted two jets fast approaching in attack position. Somehow Mitchell anticipated what would happen next—and sent his plane into a dive just as incandescent tracer bullets from one of the jets shot overhead. It was listening to his intuition that probably saved the lives of Mitchell and his crew.

But it was on *Apollo 14*'s voyage home that Mitchell had the epiphany that changed his life. Mitchell was looking at Earth through his spacecraft's small capsule window, seeing the home planet floating there in the starry depths of space, and he suddenly felt the transcendence traditionally associated with mystical experience. As he recalls in his book:

Billions of years ago the molecules of my body, of Stu's [Roosa] and Alan's [Shepard] bodies, of this spacecraft, of the world I had come from and was now returning to, were manufactured in the furnace of an ancient generation of stars like those surrounding us. . . . Our presence here, outside the domain of the home planet, was not rooted in an accident of nature or in the capricious political whim of a technological civilization. It was rather an extension of the same universal process that evolved our molecules. And what I felt was a personal connectedness with it. I experienced what has been described as an ecstasy of unity. . . . I was over-

(RIGHT) *Edgar Mitchell stands by deployed U.S. flag during early moments of the first EVA. Lunar partner Alan Shepard caught the image with a 70mm modified lunar surface Hasselblad camera.* (BELOW) *During the second EVA, Mitchell is photographed near a Modularized Equipment Transporter. (Photos courtesy of NASA.)*

whelmed with the sensation of physically and mentally extending out into the cosmos.[5]

QUANTUM METAPHYSICS

In his book, Mitchell has laid out his model for the next potential evolution of humankind. It is a "dyadic" view that holds that matter and consciousness are coupled in our universe. Mitchell maintains (and modern physics confirms) that there are limits to what the scientific model can quantify—at the subatomic level, for example, structure disappears into dynamic energy exchanges, and traditional, verifiable notions of space and time disappear. Energy itself has within it awareness and intentionality—the seeds of learning, he believes. In his dyadic model existence, knowing, awareness, and intention are inextricably related, and the physical structure of the universe and "all mentality" arose together, interconnected through the "feedback process" of learning. As human beings, we all are accountable participants in the unfolding drama of creation. We, and every living thing, are connected.

To Mitchell, the old scientific model of a universe running by immutable laws is no longer valid—a notion explored and verified in modern physics. Modern physics has also disputed the old Cartesian philosophy of Descartes (he of the memorable phrase "I think, therefore I am"), which proposed that mind and body were separate—certainly for the scientist there is no separation of the observer and the observed. In addition, the Newtonian concepts expressed by Isaac Newton in the seventeenth century held to a mechanistic view of a universe that worked like a gigantic clock with time and space as absolutes and outcomes always verifiable. These are the concepts that have driven our civilization and how we perceive ourselves and the universe—and they are old and outdated models that we cling to at our peril, Mitchell maintains.

"The factors that first led physicists to distrust their faith in a smoothly functioning mechanical universe loomed on the inner and outer horizons of knowledge—in the unseen realm of the atom and the fathomless depths of intergalactic space," Lincoln Barnett explains in his classic work *The Universe and Dr. Einstein.* "To describe these phenomena quantitatively, two great theoretical systems were developed between 1900 and 1927. One was the Quantum Theory, dealing with the fundamental units of matter and energy. The other was Relativity, dealing with space, time, and the structure of the universe as a whole."[6]

Newton himself believed that all reality was grounded in "local" forces—one body could not act upon another body through a vacuum. A modern physicist named John Stewart Bell, however, came up with his "Interconnectedness Theorem," which claims that all of reality is "nonlocal," that things can connect through space and time.

"Bell's theorem shows that although the world's phenomena seem strictly local, the reality

BEYOND SPACE AND TIME

I am out beyond our galaxy, beyond galaxies as we know them. Time is apparently speeded up 100 billion times. The whole universe collapses into a point. There is a tremendous explosion and out of the point on one side comes positive matter and positive energies, streaking into the cosmos at fantastic velocities. Out of the opposite side of the point comes antimatter streaking off into the opposite direction. The universe expands to its maximum extent, recollapses, and expands three times. During each expansion the guides say, "Man appears here and disappears there." All I can see is a thin slice for man. I ask, "Where does man go when he disappears until he is ready to reappear again?" They say, "That is us."

—DR. JOHN C. LILLY, THE CENTRE OF THE CYCLONE, 1972

The above quote comes from Dr. Lilly's personal record of isolation tank experiments he'd undertaken during the years 1964–65 while under the influence of LSD. At the time the hallucinatory drug was still legal, a situation that changed soon after Lilly's experience with deep space voyages and discarnate entities. All researchers using the substance for investigatory purposes were asked to send their supplies back to Sandoz, the chemical company that had manufactured the drug. Lilly himself was left wondering whether his experience had truly happened or whether his visions were mere phantasms of a drug-charged imagination.

But the idea of traversing the universe, of breaking the bounds of space and time, is the ultimate dream of space exploration. Theories of "wormholes" and the like—of possible interdimensional passageways instantaneously connecting impossibly distant points in the universe—are now the stuff of serious scientific conjecture. Indeed, even back in the *Lost in Space* TV series there were episodes in which alien machines magically whisked a traveler through space and time.

But the *Lost* TV show, influenced by analog technology and produced with traditional effects, was a cosmic vaudeville of wandering space cowboys and intergalactic circuses, of magical thinking machines and rusting robots, of alien fishing holes. In the new *LS* the Robinsons find themselves on a planet riddled with time portals, kaleidoscopic dimensional pathways in which some of the crew literally confront themselves as they would exist in an alternate future—it's the universe of the new physics, where mechanical views of space and time are shattered.

In 1997's *Contact*, computer graphics allowed that film to open with an incredible journey out of the solar system and close with a ride through one of those interdimensional pathways of space. Artist Ralph

Drawings copyright © by Ralph McQuarrie

McQuarrie was one of the concept artists hired by the *Contact* producers to come up with the look of the alien machine built by earthlings using blueprints transmitted from an extraterrestrial civilization. Like the old *Lost in Space* "matter transfer" machine, this device was designed to take a human astronaut beyond space and time. Although the film ultimately went with a different look, McQuarrie came up with an intriguing concept for the *Contact* machine.

"'We need an alien machine,' is what they told me," McQuarrie smiles. "They [the producers] outlined this fantastic concept of projecting a human being into space. I had the idea that if you could isolate a person in a superdense container and then send a beam through it, you could pick up the essence of this person's structure, perhaps a re-creation or clone of the psyche, and project that out into space.

"So I came up with this image of a gigantic underground cone which projected up through a lake of pure quartz. The cone was this immense, monumental object that weighed more than half the Earth. To enter it you had to move through yards and yards of this solid structure, this new supercompact material that had been invented. And I described an event in which this big laser beam would shoot from this thing and project out."

McQuarrie recalls being attracted to space as a kid growing up in Billings, Montana. In that rural environment he was able to see

Drawings copyright © by Ralph McQuarrie

"zillions" of stars in the sky. Growing up, he was dazzled by both the real-life drama of rocket scientists figuring out how to launch craft into space and Buck Rogers fantasies of space travel. "I've seen spacecraft in dreams before," he says. "I came into the world when spacecraft was very much in people's consciousness."

His imagination has taken him on many artistic flights of fancy, as he's literally dreamed up some of the off-world visions in his motion picture work. One of his dreams became a classic movie image—the gigantic mother ship depicted in director Steven Spielberg's *Close Encounters of the Third Kind* (1977). "I don't know that there isn't a collective consciousness, a sort of God consciousness, from which come very clear dreams that can predict the future," he wonders. "But I had a dream that actually preceded my work on *Close Encounters*.

"In my dream I found myself at my parents' house in Seattle, when I had this premonition to go outside. It was one of those gray, overcast Seattle days, but when I looked up I saw this cylindrical equipment hanging down out of the clouds. It was a spacecraft! I was about to jump through a hedge to get a neighbor when I heard this voice, like the voice of God, in my head saying: 'Stop where you are and go back in your house and forget that you saw this! And you will forget.' So I went back into the house and sat down. And then I awakened.

"It was a tremendously realistic dream, but I did forget it. Years later, when I was doing the sketches of the mother ship for *Close Encounters*, I didn't remember it. But when I was in the screening room and I saw the spaceship in the final film—*then* it all came back! I'd reproduced the mother ship of my dream. I suppose I violated the command not to talk about what I saw. We made a film about it and completely blew the whole secret."

McQuarrie had another seminal dream, years before his concept work on *Star Wars*. He has wondered if this fantastic dream is what opened up the floodgates of his imagination. "I imagined myself at home in Los Angeles,

sitting in my kitchen by an open window. It was night and I went out through the open window, flew over the city, and then out into outer space. As I flew past stars I could zoom in and out of passing planets, seeing the life-forms. I felt very safe, at home in the universe. Then I got to the very edge of the universe. And beyond. There were no more stars, nothing left. Just total black space. And when you've passed the last of the stars you're kind of shocked that there's nothing else. It's boring! There's nothing left to know. There's no adventure. There's no more Buck Rogers.

"So I had passed through the universe and it was like a child's toy where you play with it until you're ready for something new. So I'd look into the blackness and there was nothing there. Then I'd look back to the stars from whence I'd come and there was this boring toy. You're in a place where there's no one to come and ask how you're doing or 'What's up?' That left me with a profound depression. And then I woke up.

"I realized I was back in the universe, back in the real world. I'd been out where you have consciousness but nothing to be conscious of. I'd gotten the message that life is a constant show and the ending you don't know. We're all in the moment which keeps passing and never gets there. Everything has been moving since the universe was created, unfolding since that first moment.

"I can't explain our consciousness any other way than it's like the God consciousness. Maybe it'll be explained when the first total computer with a sensory apparatus starts having dreams like us. But we'll never get inside the computer we think has consciousness. I'll never get in your mind and you'll never get into my mind.

"I understand the mechanics of how the neurons fire, the eyes work, and everything—until I get to the point where I try to understand how all this is transformed somehow into this seamless image that we're seeing. Then I get into a hall of mirrors that I can't come to the end of. How, where does it all happen? In there, somewhere in the brain. Somehow."

beneath this phenomenal surface must be superluminal," explains Nick Hebert in *Quantum Reality*.

Religions assure us that we are all brothers and sisters, children of the same deity; biologists say that we are entwined with all life-forms on this planet: our fortunes rise or fall with theirs. Now, physicists have discovered that the very atoms of our bodies are woven out of a common superluminal fabric. Not merely in physics are humans out of touch with reality; we ignore these connections at our peril. Albert Einstein, a seeker after reality all his life, had this to say concerning the illusion of separateness:

"A human being is part of the whole, called by us 'Universe'; a part limited in time and space. He experiences himself, his thoughts and feelings as something separated from the rest—a kind of optical delusion of his consciousness. . . . Our task must be to free ourselves from this prison by widening our circle of compassion to embrace all living creatures and the whole of nature in its beauty."[7]

The meaning of nonlocality can embrace everything from intuition to the possibilities of a voodoo curse—notions unsettling to those who hold to that model of a clockwork universe. But Mitchell believes he can prove his premise that all matter in the universe has consciousness, thanks to the *quantum hologram*.

The dyadic model features the notion of the quantum hologram as an invisible, informational structure indigenous to all matter itself. "This is brand-new stuff," says Mitchell. "There are papers being written now on how simple cells use the quantum hologram to learn and to adapt to the environment. This model shows we live in a learning universe, even at the level of DNA and cell structure itself. And the quantum hologram is the nonlocal component of matter. Mystics have been saying for a thousand years or more that the universe is interconnected—well, here's the mechanism by which that takes place.

"A classical hologram is made by splitting a laser beam and focusing one portion of it on an object, recombining the beam so that the interference pattern between the object and non-object-bearing beam carries the information about the object—you focus a laser light on a photographic plate and have a free-standing hologram of an object. It's the image of the object, it's not there. What we're saying is that in nature each object has associated and resonate with it, its own hologram. This helps to explain all the mystical phenomena discussed in religious literature and also precisely why the intuitive function works in the brain. You could call it the mind of God. Absolutely."

MESSAGES FROM SPACE

In the following exchange, Mitchell expounds on his theory of consciousness, his memories of space travel, and the future of manned space missions.

Your vision of Earth when returning from the Moon is what really kicked off your continuing journey into the nature of consciousness. But I sense that you would have been exploring these issues regardless.
MITCHELL: Well, some of us [astronauts] were deeply affected by our experiences. I happen to

have the philosophical mind-set that I went into some of these issues very deeply.

The epiphany I had in space is what got me started. My first reaction was, what kind of brain *is* this? Why does the brain permit, or cause, an epiphany that is accompanied by a "Wow," then an integration of information, then an acceleration to go along with it? Why does that happen? We've been doing this since we've been reflective humans, which is only about 3,500 years. When you look at the natural evolutionary phenomenon that causes it, it blows you away. Then you suddenly realize we've had the wrong slant on it all along. You change your viewpoint a little bit, and my God, it all falls into place.

It's interesting that even before you had your epiphany in space you already showed an interest in the nature of consciousness by arranging your ESP experiments before the launch of your Apollo mission. Did this interest come as an outgrowth of your professional training or in spite of it?
MITCHELL: Probably in spite of it, because our culture has not encouraged us to be intuitive. But we all use our intuitive faculties.

It seems that the early, optimistic dream of space travel has been replaced by fear.
MITCHELL: Well, the fear is because we recognize, even if it's only from the gut level, that our infrastructure is falling apart, that there's something strange going on here. It's a deep, intuitive recognition, just as I had when I was in space, that the way we're thinking about ourselves is wrong. That's why I set out to find out what is a right model. That's what [the late mythologist] Joseph Campbell was saying—we need a new myth about ourselves. So I produced a new myth.

Could you elaborate on the nature of your dyadic model?
MITCHELL: My whole thesis is that Western civilization is built upon the Cartesian duality and classical

Newtonian science—and it's flawed! It's wrong. It's that simple. Science has been wrong in dismissing things like intuition as part of the human experience, and the mystical side has been wrong in ascribing it to divine or satanic forces.

You don't have to look "Out There" for personal decisions and morality. Because *this* is the only thing we've got! That's exactly what the dyadic model is. It says we have an existing universe and we experience it. And how do we experience it? Because we have consciousness. It is being aware. Our intention, our volition, counts for something.

You're saying we have to listen to our inner sense in order to make intelligent decisions?
MITCHELL: Well, that's the phenomenon of the aware, intelligent organism. Intelligence is simply the ability to manage information, and that's the "Wow" of our universe. This is an intelligent universe. It not only exists, it has intelligence. It's self-organizing. And when you say "self-organizing," you're getting right back to the primacy of the first-person experience. We're able to be aware and now, as an evolved species, self-reflectively aware. My argument is that awareness or perception has to be inherent in matter itself. And the essence of this is the first-person experience. We only know what we experience from our very evolved, complex state.

Science has to recognize that there is no objective experience without a first-person experience. In

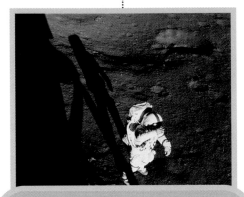

(ABOVE) *Shepard appears to shade his eyes from the glare of the Sun in this image photographed by Mitchell.*
(BELOW) *The* Apollo 14 *lunar module reflects the Sun in a brilliant ball of light the lunar-walking astronauts described as having a "jewel-like appearance." (Photos courtesy of NASA.)*

other words, subjectivity is the basis of all experience and you can't get around that! I can say "they," because I'm a "me." So on the practical level, consciousness is a first-person experience and you're never going to understand consciousness until you understand the first-person experience. My model is an energy and informational model, and information is the key. That's exactly what our brains do—organize information.

By "first-person experience," you're referring to states such as intuition and extrasensory perception?
MITCHELL: Those are all first-person experiences. We must have an inner experience first, before we can know about an outer experience. Inner experiences are also trainable capabilities, particularly if you start young enough. You can train what might be called the Christ force right into a child if you go about it properly. But first one has to believe that it can be done, that we have these unlimited capabilities, that mind *does* influence matter. It's exactly the whole notion that God isn't without us—it's within!

So, psychic, even spiritual, phenomena are evident by the issue of the "nonlocality" in quantum mechanics?
MITCHELL: Quantum nonlocality has been demonstrated in the laboratory and shows that once particles are in the same process they remain quantum-correlated throughout the universe, regardless of where they are. Since all processes

were, at the moment of the Big Bang, in the same process, that means they have remained quantum-correlated throughout all time—and the quantum hologram is the way that takes place. Now, what that means is what we call our sixth sense, which classical science has disregarded, *is really the first sense*. It was nature's information management tool long before the environment developed, before we developed our five normal sensory mechanisms.

So what we're saying is that all of nature has a mechanism that resonates with each object. Each object has its own hologram. Each object hologram carries its own history. It's the essence, the spiritual side if you will, of the physical object. It is responsible for our nonlocal knowing about things, for all the intuitive, telepathic, and clairvoyant content of information we humans seem to experience from beyond the local organism.

The sixth sense is simply picking up nonlocal information—sensitive people such as mystics, psychics, and shamans have been using it all along. I like the analogy that television and radio waves are coursing through our bodies right now, and unless you happen to have braces on your teeth you're not going to pick them up—there are people who pick up radio waves on their bridgework! The quantum hologram is going through all of us all the time and we do have the machinery to pick that up, if we're trained and haven't let our neuroconnections atrophy. That is exactly what intuition and

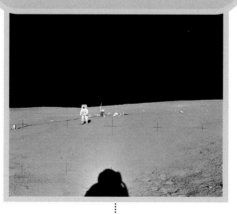

(ABOVE) *Shepard, with lunar dust clinging to his space suit, stands by a Moon boulder.* (BELOW) *Mitchell, at work in the lunar distance, with foreground shadow of Shepard taking the picture. (Photos courtesy of NASA.)*

psychic functioning is all about—picking up nonlocal information. And the quantum hologram is the mechanism for that.

How should the average person open himself to this new way of seeing?

MITCHELL: People have to get educated about what science is telling us about the world today and also be open to the inner, first-person experience, and the fact that we each have a choice. That is a fundamental step. And it is an awesome responsibility to suddenly be responsible for everything you do, and to collectively be responsible for the fate of the species and the planet itself. And that's what we are.

Learning, which is what everyone does, is simply a feedback loop that incorporates volition and awareness. And my argument is that volition and awareness are natural attributes of the way the universe has structured itself. We've denied this in the past. Even animals have volition and awareness—you can trace this learning loop all the way down the level of complexity to the simplest organisms. And since it's indigenous to the universe itself, it must trace on down even into inanimate objects.

If it's an intelligently self-organizing universe, then knowledge—and I mean proper, verifiable knowledge—has to be linked together into a holistic picture of what we are and how we fit into the cosmos. The human condition is that we're all going to make interpretations according to our experience, and the broader the experience, the simpler it becomes. In other words, when you have the God knowledge, everything looks very simple.

How do you use intuition in your own life?

MITCHELL: I use it in my daily life all the time—we all do. We're all intuitive, we all pick up hunches that we listen to or not. Sometimes you'll have an instant like or dislike of someone you just met. Why? Is it intrinsic to them, is it because that person reminds you of someone else, are you comparing that person to a memory? This is all part of the mystery of how the mind/brain works. But this type of very holographic information is vital to how that functions.

If your dyadic model of consciousness is accepted, do you foresee the old institutions falling away?

MITCHELL: Absolutely. The institutions will just change form. We can see right now that the institutions we've constructed based upon Newtonian and Cartesian reality are falling apart. They're inadequate to the task. So, it's got to go through a change. And if you look at systems theory you'll see that the whole system is far from equilibrium and it's about to reach a bifurcation point. The Soviet Union went through one and experienced a massive change. We *are* going through a massive change. How fast we're going to go through it, and which way it'll all go, has yet to be determined.

The main driving force is that the world's population in the last forty years has doubled from three billion to six billion. And it's going to come close to doubling again in the next thirty to forty years. And if the institutions don't change to accommodate that, we've really got ourselves a problem. We'll be able to solve our problems if we stop the consumption ethic and start living in tune with nature, using our technologies for our mutual benefit and the benefit of the planet, not for self-serving ego ventures and simply building personal wealth.

Is a change in our consciousness, how we perceive ourselves and the universe, necessary for our future evolution?

MITCHELL: The first evolution is rethinking who we are, and the absolute mind-blowing revelation of the fact of how we are self-reflectively aware beings. We've gone through all these explanations of other dimensions, of discarnate deities creating the universe. It's a myth. The universe is exactly what we see it is, what we're experiencing right now. This is it! The only difference is the universe has its own intelligence and we're in it for better or for worse. It's a pretty amazing place that we live in. We just happen to not be seeing that. The personal metaphor is to get the left and the right hemispheres of the brain more coherent.

So, as we evolve, will we move away from duality, of seeing things in terms of "good" and "bad" and the like?

MITCHELL: No. It's all still a process. We'll always make mistakes. Learning is a trial-and-error process. Anyone who gets hung up on the fact that people make mistakes and can go off on wild tangents is just denying the process itself. When you're creating the future there's no assurance that what you're creating is going to survive or succeed. We're always operating on less than total information.

In a sense, are we already undergoing this evolution in consciousness? Is it the nature of our species to try to correct our mistakes?

MITCHELL: Exactly. This is our choice. To either correct this mistake or have it go uncorrected, in which case nature will correct it for us, perhaps to our detriment. There's no reason why our species should survive. It's our choice. But nature doesn't let you survive if your mistakes are too dramatic, if you overpopulate, which we are; if you're too consumption-oriented, which we are; if you pollute, which we're doing. Even birds don't foul their own nests!

We're polluting and frivolously using up resources. And there's no need for it.

Some would say that your ability to get to the Moon was predicated on the same technology that's no longer valid.
MITCHELL: Yeah.

Are they right or wrong in that opinion?
MITCHELL: Well, all of our technology is built upon itself, what we discover. Science progresses by discovering anomalies in the current models. If the current models work and get us somewhere, then they're OK. It's just that they're incomplete. And what we've discovered through anomalies is how to get another portion of completeness. But do we know the final answer? No. We haven't created it yet.

So future space missions will invent new ways of propulsion and so on?
MITCHELL: Sure.

Spacecraft will look different?
MITCHELL: Absolutely. No question about it. The technology of the *Apollo* era looks totally archaic compared to the technology of today.

Did you have Buck Rogers dreams of space travel when you were a child?
MITCHELL: No, I didn't. I'm a meat-and-potatoes guy. But I'm also the sort of guy who's curious. I'm an explorer. The track of the explorer is to go deeper and try to find out the answers when things aren't

(ABOVE) *The* Apollo 14 *lunar module in ascent stage, the engine creating a burst of wind that stirs the lunar dust and shakes the American flag. Photo taken from a 16mm camera mounted inside the lunar module.* (BELOW) *In the early morning hours of February 12, 1971, safely returned to Earth, the* Apollo 14 *astronauts gaze out from the glass of their Mobile Quarantine Facility (with Shepard and Roosa peering close to the window). (Photos courtesy of NASA.)*

fitting for you. I want to know what's next. I think my heritage is very relevant to how and why all this happened to me. My folks made me very independent and questioning and appreciative of the intricacies of nature.

My desire to go into space didn't come until after *Sputnik* went up. Then when President Kennedy announced the *Apollo* program I knew that's where I would be.

You've said that it's our destiny to journey into space.
MITCHELL: Yes, and we will in due course. Now, this next century is going to be a bear as we go through all of this restructuring [of society]. But I doubt if there'll be a manned trip to Mars in the next thirty years.

It seemed you must have needed a steely nerve to successfully complete a mission to the Moon.
MITCHELL: There was no fear.

Did that attitude come from your astronaut training?
MITCHELL: Well, if you aren't trained to be that way, you shouldn't be there. Does that mean there's not moments of apprehension? Of course there's moments of apprehension, but most of that has to do with concerns of whether you're up to the task.

I ask that because if it's our destiny as a species to voyage into space, do we all have to begin preparing ourselves in a certain way?

MITCHELL: Aren't we already doing that by looking at things like *Star Trek* and *Star Wars*, all of these space-type things, as far-fetched as some of them are? Isn't that what we're preparing people for?

You mentioned how revelatory it was to return to Earth from the Moon. What was the feeling like when you were first launched into space?
MITCHELL: It was like climbing to the top of a mountain and getting a new view. I felt it as an awesome, wonderful, exciting, ebullient experience.

How do you prepare for something as unique as being launched into outer space?
MITCHELL: Intellectually you look at the photos that have been taken, you look at a globe of Earth, and you say it's going to look like that [from space]—but real! You prepare yourself in exactly those ways and then you go and do it. You just experience it.

It's been twenty-five years since human beings have walked on the Moon. It seems as if we've pulled back from manned space travel.
MITCHELL: Well, that's okay. But we have the messages from there. Most of us who went to the Moon, or have even been in space, have said if we could ever get politicians to look at Earth from out there in space we would have a different order of reality.

What will trigger our next manned outer space voyage?
MITCHELL: Enough political will and public insight to recognize that it has to be done.

In your book you state: "The promise of our technologies lies in our eventual escape from a dying planet." Do you mean "dying planet" in terms of what we're doing to it, or that our natural evolution is to leave our planet?

Astronaut Edgar Mitchell. (Photo courtesy of NASA.)

MITCHELL: Well, either or both. If we kill our planet we'll have to eventually escape it. Ultimately the planet is going to survive with or without us.

The Pathfinder mission sent back amazing images from the surface of Mars. Do you think this mission will generate renewed public interest in the space program?
MITCHELL: Sure, because we're getting a broader perspective of ourselves. The main thing is for us to stop being parochial. We've been parochial in terms of our tribal thought, in terms of our city-state thought. And we've sure as hell been parochial in terms of our planetary thought. We've got to transcend all of that and start to see from what we term the "God perspective." The cosmic perspective.

So will our culture turn back to the exploration of outer space?
MITCHELL: I think so. We will. As soon as you start to see how [reality] is, instead of how we thought it was, all things are possible. But you've got to get past that fear. You've got to get the perception of 'The All That Is.'"

THE RETURN OF THE TIME TRAVELER

It's been a long journey from those Third Eye days when popular culture was still full of innocence and wonder. The business side was safely hidden behind the curtain. Movie and TV visual effects work was still a mysterious craft, with nameless artists producing visual miracles. *Lost in Space* came out of that era when the marvelous "future" had not yet fully arrived.

Kids in particular, not yet jaded by routine space shuttle launches or by visual mediums charged up with photorealistic digital effects, could get lost in *Lost in Space*: The distant vista of an alien landscape was a vision of wonder, not a painted backdrop; alien monsters were weird and scary, not guys in creature suits; and there went the *Jupiter 2* zooming through space, not a model flying on wires.

Lost in Space was part of a let's-put-on-a-show era. Our friend Bob Burns not only worked in that era (such as on *Invasion of the Saucer-Men*) but was a true showman of that more innocent time. For years Burns's Burbank driveway and back yard became transformed every Halloween into a staging ground for what he's called "live illusion shows." Thousands came every Halloween to be thrilled by visual effects spectacles, usually re-creating scary moments from such fantasy and science fiction films as *Forbidden Planet*, *This Island Earth*, and *War of the Worlds*.

Old pros like Jim Danforth and rising young effects artists such as future Academy Award winners Rick Baker and Dennis Muren (who supervised ILM's full-motion dinosaurs in both *Jurassic Park* and *Lost World*) joined in to put on a show, with Burns overseeing the whole enterprise of what *Starlog* magazine once called a "Hollywood Halloween."

The "Bob Burns and Friends" Hollywood Halloween shows at Burns's Burbank home were a seasonal delight—and quite a sight for astonished neighbors. (TOP RIGHT) *A view of 30-foot Martian spaceship that, by effects magic, appears to have crashed into the back of Burns's home, just in time for the 1975* War of the Worlds *show.* (RIGHT) *The "Goombah" crawls over Burns's rooftop in this 1970 Halloween sighting.*

(TOP) *Early in their careers some of today's effects industry veterans practiced their craft at the Burns Halloween shows. In this 1971 shot, the crew for* The Return of Mr. Hyde *show pose with props* (FROM LEFT TO RIGHT): *Jon Berg, Bob Burns, Bill Hedge, Tom Scherman, and Dennis Muren.* (ABOVE) *Charlie Dugdale and crew lead Robby the Robot in battle against the infamous "Id" monster in a 1973* Forbidden Planet *Halloween show.*

The shows had been a Burbank tradition since 1967, when Burns began fixing up his living room into a haunted house or a Dr. Frankenstein's lab—all the better to dazzle neighborhood trick-or-treaters. From there he and his buddies from the Hollywood visual FX industry went on to create such elaborate backyard productions as a meticulous re-creation of the *Nostromo* spaceship from *Alien*.

Burns's expanding collection of pop cultural artifacts finally forced him to fill up that backyard with a museum to house his treasures. The Hollywood Halloween tradition ended with a 1982 *Creature from the Black Lagoon* production. "I miss doing the shows," Burns says wistfully. "I loved Halloween when I was a kid, and I'd just get so sick hearing these stories about trick-or-treaters getting candy with razor blades in them. I wanted to show kids that Halloween could be fun. We had a lot of fun on those shows. The cream of the crop of effects artists and prop builders worked on them. They were live illusion shows which had to work the first time in front of an audience."

One of Burns's favorite Halloween productions was 1976's "The Return of the Time Traveler," which ran for two nights and almost 50 shows, playing to almost 4,000 people. The star was the Time Machine itself, that actual prop from the George Pal movie that Burns had spent years tracking down. The show was a spectacle of lights, recorded sounds, a narrator describing the action, and a fantastic effects set built with rotating walls for a live time-traveling effect.

On a raised stage, the Time Machine was placed in a set of the time traveler's Victorian study. Dennis Muren, who at the time had been working as an effects cameraman on the first *Star Wars*, came up with lighting effects, in particular a light burst designed to show a mishap on the way to the future, with all the light effects playing off a gossamer theatrical scrim placed between the stage and the audience. The entire voyage to the future was realized within seconds, with the rotating set walls turned around and the lights dimmed to magically reveal the dark cave of the Morlocks—who would be lurking in the shadows.

Pal's movie had originally ended with the time traveler taking from his library three mysterious books, then hopping back into the Time Machine to return to the aid of the gentle Eloi and Weena, the woman of the future he loved. "It was always a big question—'What were the three books?'" Burns asks rhetorically. "Actually George Pal didn't know the three books either."

But while Pal's movie ended with the time traveler having disappeared into the future, Burns and his crew came up with a macabre twist on what might have happened. "As the time traveler sits in the Machine and starts to head into the future, there's a big starburst explosion in space and time which knocks him off course, causing him to land not outside but *inside* the cave of the Morlocks," Burns says. "Dennis had this big strobe light that momentarily blinded the audience with this big flash that hit the scrim and turned it a brilliant white.

"By then the lights fade up and you see the time traveler is in the cave of the Morlocks. The time traveler finds a human skull. And he doesn't see about eight Morlocks creeping up behind him! They close in around him and the narrator goes: 'They want to feed—ON OUR FLESH!' Then we did a 'Boo': As the lights came up, three of the Morlocks ran through the audience!"

Burns remembers that the highlight of the "Time Traveler" show was when George Pal himself visited the set. "We sat George in the Time Machine and took a picture of him at the controls—it became his favorite photograph," Burns says, smiling. "It was the first time he had sat in it! When he was making the movie he'd never thought of doing that because he was so busy making the film. But years later, sitting in the Time Machine, he was like a little kid."

Back in 1980 Burns was asked by *Starlog* magazine why Hollywood professionals would donate their time and Burns handle the expenses (which often ran into the thousands of dollars) for an old-fashioned backyard illusion show. "Mainly . . . it's love," he replied. "A love of make-believe."[8]

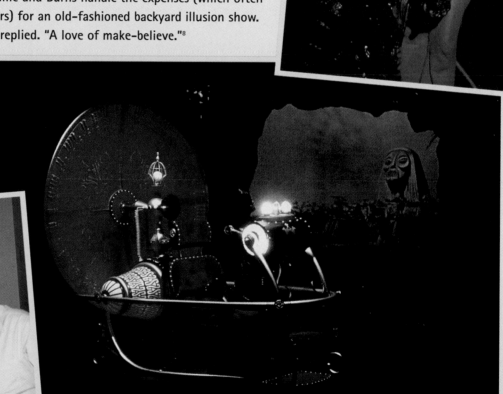

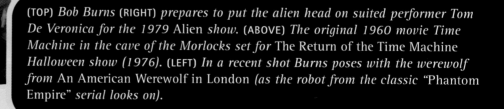

(TOP) *Bob Burns* (RIGHT) *prepares to put the alien head on suited performer Tom De Veronica for the 1979* Alien *show.* (ABOVE) *The original 1960 movie Time Machine in the cave of the Morlocks set for* The Return of the Time Machine Halloween *show (1976).* (LEFT) *In a recent shot Burns poses with the werewolf from* An American Werewolf in London *(as the robot from the classic "Phantom Empire" serial looks on).*

U.S. Astronaut Frank Borman joins in honoring space pioneer Yuri Gagarin, the "first explorer of the mysteries of space," as noted in a 1977 Soviet publication. (©Novosti Press Agency Publishing House, 1977) A tradition for returning cosmonauts was to visit Star Town and place flowers at the Gagarin memorial statue.

12 THE WAY HOME

Are we, as the fabled twenty-first century approaches, still innocent enough to dream of escape into either the future or the realms of other stars? Or has the future come too close to escape to, and are the stars revealed as, in all their random splendor, out of reach?

—JOHN UPDIKE, THE NEW YORKER, FEBRUARY 26, 1990

We're settlers, not explorers.

—MAUREEN ROBINSON IN "THE DERELICT," LOST IN SPACE EPISODE TWO, SEASON ONE, 1965

The 1997 *Mir* space station debacle was something out of an early George Pal outer space adventure, a drama of man and machine set in the vastness of outer space.

Two Russians and one American were aboard when disaster struck. Cosmonaut Vasily Tsibliyev was watching a monitor of the *Progress*, a robot cargo ship, and manipulating remote-control joysticks to dock the craft. Suddenly the robot ship stopped responding to the remote signals and rammed a solar panel on the station's Spektr science module, knocking out 50 percent of the station's power, punching a hole in the hull, and destabilizing the station. The crew had to scramble to seal off the damaged module and work to overcome the life-threatening dangers, which included failing onboard systems that caused heat and humidity to rise to critical levels.

By early September blame for *Mir*'s problems was leveled at both crew and ground controllers, even as U.S. astronaut Michael Foale and cosmonaut Anatoly Solovyev completed a daring space walk for the first hands-on inspection of the damaged hull. The incident had run the emotional range from concerns about the effect of stress on decision making in outer space to the ingenuity of the Russian and American crew who answered the call of danger.

The problems of *Mir* were also laid to its age: The space station, originally planned to last just five years, was in its eleventh year of operation. The Space Age had begun in 1957 with the basketball-sized sphere *Sputnik*, which made some 1,350 orbits during its three months of operation. Forty years later, the massive *Mir* space station was completing its 65,000th orbit even as plans proceeded to have a new international space station operational by the latter part of 1998.

LOST IN SPACE

"Things go wrong in space all the time," NASA administrator Daniel Goldin told *Time* in a July 7 article covering the *Mir* accident.

Testament to the reality that sometimes settlers die on the frontier is the Space Mirror at the Kennedy Space Center, the memorial to astronauts who have died in the line of duty. Looking like the mysterious black monolith of *2001*, the Mirror, a slab of black granite more than forty feet high and

This view of the Mir Spektr *module reveals the damage to the solar panel and other areas that occurred when a resupply ship collided with the space station. (Photo courtesy of NASA.)*

that first U.S. space walk)—was still two years away.

The fictional crew of the *Jupiter 2*, reflecting the can-do optimism of the time, met their own fate with unfailing spirit. Even Dr. Smith, who was constantly scheming and praying to return to Earth, had a rare epiphany when, after contemplating the challenges posed by the planet on which they were marooned, exulted to John Robinson: "Before you know it we'll be off into the heavens, an infinitely better people for our ordeal, conditioned to survive in any kind of environment, toughened by our encounter with alien life-forms. . . . "

They're lost out there still, on the endless voyage to Alpha Centauri. The adventures of the space-traveling Robinsons are little time capsules from the early Space Age. The wonder of the unfolding future is there, the valiant family unit is intact, the all-American values are still triumphant and able to bravely suffer even the twisted schemes of a Dr. Smith.

But sometimes the perils took their toll. There was the time when the spirit of an alien warrior took possession of John Robinson's body. The commander, with the love of his son, would exorcise the alien, but not before a fevered battle within himself. It was a rare moment in which the stoic space leader let down his guard and expressed regret. "In many ways you're a better son than I am a father," he said to Will as he was wracked by fever.

John Robinson then confessed to Maureen that he regretted taking Will, Penny, and Judy out into space. "There's so much they haven't experienced," he choked, realizing the price they'd all paid in leaving Mother Earth behind in search of a new world, a new home.

But if the Robinson children felt terror or angst at their predicament, they rarely showed it.

fifty feet wide, always rotates with its back to the sun, allowing sunlight to glow through the letters of the more than a dozen names carved completely through the slab.

The view of manned space travel during the mid- to late nineties is markedly different from the cocky, gung-ho superman astronaut imagined in the fifties. Back then it was a given that man would not just walk on the moon within a decade but soon after plant a flag of conquest on alien worlds and set up colonies throughout the solar system.

By the time *Lost in Space* made its debut in 1965, the vision had come a bit more into focus. Man had still not ventured out past Earth's gravitational pull, but there were already satellites and manned spaceships orbiting the planet and men walking in space. The first true disaster for the U.S. space program—the launching pad fire that killed astronauts Grissom, Chaffee, and White (who made

For Penny, a strange new world was another place in which to be blissfully alone with her imagination. For Judy it was all so romantic, feeling the glow of an alien twilight and trying to catch the eye of the rugged young Major West.

For Will it was heaven to have an entire universe in which to indulge his insatiable curiosity, his love of tinkering, his physical joy in striking out for the unseen vistas beyond the next alien hill. Will saw the universe through the eyes of boyhood innocence.

There was the time, not long after the *Jupiter 2* had been knocked off course, that he and Dr. Smith encountered a monstrous-looking being that dwelled within a lost alien ship. Smith was quick to raise his blaster, but Will was quicker to caution: "They're not like us—but maybe they are." (The Robinsons would later joke about how ironic it was to come across another ship that seemed to be as lost in space as they were.)

Will simply knew no fear. Whether out in the dark void of space or on an alien world, the universe held no terrors for young Robinson. It was on one of the worlds they'd reached on their wanderings that Will met Marvello, ringmaster of the marvelous space circus. Will listened wide-eyed as the nomadic ringmaster told the boy of a glittering planet with four moons that cast a silvery light, an asteroid where multicolored fish swam in rivers of light, a world with mountain ranges made of diamonds—and he wanted to go to those exotic places.

When Will discovered an alien "matter transfer unit" on the first world on which they were stranded, he fearlessly saw the opportunity to transport himself to Earth to alert Alpha Control to his family's predicament. The situation was dire, since bumbling Dr. Smith had also left the cap off a bottle of carbon tetrachloride, a food preservative that left the camp's food supply vulnerable.

Without telling anyone, Will slipped out to the alien machine with his loyal Robot companion. Will arranged for the Robot to send out the signals that would send him to Earth on a beam of light and return him three hours later. When the beam of light shone on the boy, he disappeared, instantly cutting through ten light-years of space and time and dropping on a snowy rooftop in a small Vermont town.

Since it'd been many months since the ill-fated *Jupiter 2* mission was launched, Will would discover it was 1998—but we know it as the alternate future envisioned in 1965. This little Vermont town was like a living lithographic tableau devised by Currier and Ives, seemingly untouched by Space Age technology.

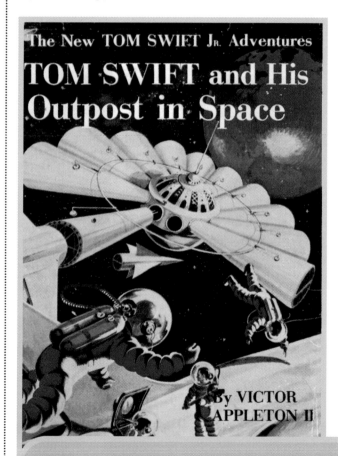

Before the journey into space there was the dream— and in dreams the likes of Tom Swift Jr. were already building outposts in space. (Tom Swift and his Outpost in Space, cover art. Grosset & Dunlap, Inc. ©1955)

JUNE LOCKHART

rom her classic TV roles in *Lassie* and *Lost in Space*, the name June Lockhart has become synonymous with the title "America's Mom," a truly all-American combination of earth mother and beauty queen. But the Lockhart name is also embossed five times over on stars on the Hollywood Walk of Fame, honoring June (with two stars), her father (two stars), and her mother, Kathleen.

In the years since Lockhart's famous TV roles, she's devoted considerable energy to public events and civic causes—"the best use of celebrity," she says. In the *Lost in Space* year of 1997, June rode on the Edison Company's float in the Rose Parade (the legendary inventor introduced her parents to one another) and was busy as an official ambassador for the California State Parks System.

But Lockhart truly lights up when she describes a passionate lifelong interest in the magic of human-powered flight, particularly the adventure of space travel. She beams when she describes how her father's song, "The World Is Waiting for the Sunrise," was played to awaken the astronauts on a *Columbia* shuttle flight while she was in attendance at Mission Control at the Johnson Space Center in Houston (the Lockhart tune even "awakened" the probe *Sojourner* on Mars).

Lockhart takes pride in the fact that she was the first woman in space—at least as far as the television medium—and traces her earliest interest in flights of fancy to such childhood memories as a love of the Sunday comic adventures of *Flash Gordon*. She especially identified with Dale Arden, Flash's adventurous fiancée. "I wanted to be Dale Arden," she laughs. "I realized during the second season of *Lost in Space* that I was actually fulfilling an early fantasy of mine. I *was* Dale Arden. I'd made it! What a hoot!"

Noting that NASA has had a direct impact on American life, Lockhart checks off a long list of products originally developed by private industry for the space program which have reached the civilian population, including: medical breakthroughs from MRIs and CAT scans to pacemakers, laser technologies for medical applications, computers, satellites designed for communications and weather prediction, robotics, advances in food processing, lightweight equipment for firefighters, water purification systems, cushioned athletic shoes, corrosion-resistant paints, and even scratch-proof polymer material for dark glass lenses. "It's not all Velcro, baby," Lockhart laughs.

June enthusiastically relates her earliest memories of flight and her ongoing love affair with the U.S. space program.

I can still remember standing out on my front lawn on Long Island watching those little bi-planes fly over when I was a child. It was just magic to me. When I started flying commercially, that was just a miracle—I never sleep on a plane in case I miss something. In the late forties, I did public relations for Western Airlines when they were opening up their routes up and down the West Coast with their DC-4s. I've flown in hot air balloons. I've also flown in gliders which are really wonderful; you're towed aloft by a single engine plane that leaves you up there and you just soar for as long as the wind lasts. So I've always been very intrigued and excited by the space program—space is hot!

I vividly remember being on the set of Lassie and doing a scene in a pickup truck when John Glenn made his flight. Now, there's a period of time on reentry when you lose radio communication with the space capsule, so I turned to little Jon Provost and quietly said I was going to go to the dressing room and I'd be back when Glenn landed. Everybody on the set was interested, but we had a director who could care less. So I excused myself to go to the ladies' room and left the soundstage, went to my dressing room, and turned on the radio. I didn't come back to the set until I'd heard that Glenn and his capsule had safely landed in the ocean.

I've had many visits to NASA. Give yourself a treat and go down to Houston to see the new space station they're building [scheduled for launch in 1998]. It's HUGE! You're dwarfed by it. It's just the most overwhelming thing imaginable. On the tour, they take you to a huge pool that's in a building the size of an airplane hangar to see the astronauts practice their EVAs (extra vehicular activities). Walking underwater simulates zero gravity of space, and they're there working with this equipment in their bulky uniforms wearing huge gloves. When you're visiting and chatting with these guys, you feel as if they're twenty-one feet tall. But astronauts today are not just Top Gun flyboy hotshots. We've sent up astronomers, physicians, engineers—they're the most wonderfully educated men and women.

During my visit, some of these astronauts and people working at the pool said watching **Lost in Space** made them know what they wanted to do when they grew up. That boggled my mind because it was just a Wednesday night show on CBS with actors reading their lines. But what a wonderful thing to be part of, to think people were making career choices while watching the show! It just sparked people's imaginations.

June Lockhart, lost in space . . . and back on Earth.

I was invited to watch the February 3, 1994, launch of the space shuttle **Discovery** at Cape Canaveral in Florida, which was the first time we took a Russian up with us. Going to the launch was wonderful. There were press conferences and events leading up to the 7 AM lift-off. Time means nothing down there; everything is round-the-clock.

Interestingly enough, I realized during the launch that the noise was about as loud as the earthquake we'd recently experienced in Los Angeles in January of that year. You're watching from a couple miles away, but the whole terrain shakes! The flames from the thrusters are shot into this **huge** pool of water, which they've been using since the early launches when the cement area underneath would get so badly burned it would have to be rebuilt. Now they release thousands of pounds of water underneath the thrusters which causes this steam to be released. They had no idea how exciting this would look!

Then there's that moment, as the ground shakes underneath you and the gimbals are moving, that you think, "Is this going to go?" And then off it goes, up, up, up, and it starts into its trajectory. And as this tiny thing goes overhead, you realize how vulnerable the astronauts are. It's heart-stopping. But until you get the separation of the thrusters and the shuttle, everybody's very quiet because that's the most dangerous moment, the moment when the **Challenger** disaster occurred. When the announcer says, "We have separation," the cheers go up and you see this thing go off into the blue. And then you breathe, with tears streaming down your cheeks.

In July of '94 I was down at the Houston Space Center for the twenty-fifth anniversary of the **Apollo 11** moon landing. During this visit the protocol lady told me, "We have a treat for you today—they're going to invite you on the floor of Mission Control." I just thought, "My God, how marvelous." Then they asked me if I would like to speak to the astronauts on the shuttle **Columbia.** I couldn't believe it! I made the telephone connection and I talked to the commander, Bob Cabana. I heard his voice saying, "Hello, June." And I said, "I'm not lost in space anymore. I'm right here in Mission Control!"

The Lost in Space cast—classic TV show and feature film incarnations.
(ABOVE, LEFT TO RIGHT): *Major Don West (Matt LeBlanc), Judy Robinson (Heather Graham), Penny Robinson (Lacey Chabert), Maureen Robinson (Mimi Rogers), Will Robinson (Jack Johnson), John Robinson (William Hurt), Dr. Zachary Smith (Gary Oldman), the Robot.*
(OPPOSITE, LEFT TO RIGHT): *Major Don West (Mark Goddard), Maureen Robinson (June Lockhart), John Robinson (Guy Williams), Will Robinson (Bill Mumy), Penny Robinson (Angela Cartwright), Dr. Zachary Smith (Jonathan Harris), Judy Robinson (Marta Kristen), the Robot (performer, Bob May, voice, Dick Tufeld).*

It was Christmastime, and snow blanketed a village absent of automobiles. Stillness hung in the air like a morning fog. Homes and stores were decorated with simple Christmas wreaths and trees. The brick and wood buildings had wood-burning stoves, old-fashioned telephones, and not a TV set in sight. Even a local reporter carried with him an old-time newsroom flash camera.

The townspeople thought Will, who kept talking about the need to call Alpha Control and alert headquarters to the plight of the *Jupiter 2*, was an obviously troubled orphan boy with a wild imagination, in need of a loving home. How could he be Will Robinson when everybody knew that America's first family in space had died during that disastrous 1997 mission? "The real Will Robinson is dead," taunted an orphan boy waiting for a bus to take him to a foster home. "So are his folks. Everybody knows that. They're skeletons floating around in space."

But Will convinced Davey Sims, an older lad looking forward to majoring in physics when he got to college. Precious moments before the matter transfer beam was set to hit, Davey helped Will scramble back up onto the low-hanging, snow-covered rooftop where he'd originally landed, even buying Will a precious bottle of carbon tetrachloride to take back with him. Will could see some of the well-meaning townspeople coming after him, trying to take him away before the beam could slash through the sky and transport him back across the impossible gulf of space to the alien world where his family and friends awaited.

Only a few moments before, Will had been in Davey's room, talking to the local lad about the wonders of space.

It was crazy, the idea that this kid had crossed space and time to come to this rural town, so cozy and covered with Christmas snow. But Davey believed. And he had to know what it was like . . .

"Will you tell me about space?" Davey asked.

"Well, it's not so difficult once you find a place you can live on," Will said.

"You mean it's just like here on Earth?"

"Well, a person from Earth isn't so different, his feelings and all. And the forms of life you meet there—well, they're different to look at, and you have to watch out that they don't misunderstand your reasons for being there. But they're not so different either. Everything in the whole universe is made up of the same molecules we are, they're just rearranged differently, that's all. What you have to learn is to translate what they are into what you are."

Back at the rooftop, Davey asked Will if he could join him in the voyage through space and time. But the matter transfer unit had only been programmed for one, Will cautioned. But Will noted that perhaps the two friends would someday meet again—out there in the stars.

"Bye, Davey," Will grinned. "Merry Christmas."

And then a beam of light shone down from the heavens and took the boy away.

NOTES

INTRODUCTION

1. James Conaway, *The Smithsonian: 150 Years of Adventure, Discovery, and Wonder* (Washington, D.C.: Smithsonian Books, and New York: Alfred A. Knopf, 1995), p. 230.
2. Isaac Asimov, "Anatomy of a Man from Mars," *Esquire* (Sept. 1965), p. 113.

CHAPTER ONE: MYSTERY OF SPACE

1. Albro T. Gaul, *The Complete Book of Space Travel* (Cleveland and New York: World, 1956), p. 14
2. *Ibid.*, p. 49.

CHAPTER TWO: THIRD EYE CULTURE

1. Jules Feiffer, *The Great Comic Book Heroes* (New York: Dial Press, 1965), p. 189.
2. *Life* (March 11, 1966), cover.

CHAPTER FOUR:
IT'S A MAN'S UNIVERSE

1. Edward R. Murrow, "A-Bomb Mission to Moscow," *Collier's* (October 27, 1951), p. 19.
2. Hearing before the House Committee on Un-American Activities: "Communist Psychological Warfare (Brainwashing): Consultation with Edward Hunter, author and foreign correspondent" (Eighty-fifth Congress, second session, March 13, 1958), p. 7.
3. Michael Weldon, *The Psychotronic Encyclopedia of Film* (New York: Ballantine Books, 1983), p. 717.
4. Bruce Handy, "Bondmania—James Bondmania," *Spy* (October 1988), p. 80.

CHAPTER FIVE:
DANGER, WILL ROBINSON!

1. "The Touch and Steal Bandits," *Flash* #150 (Feb. 1965).

CHAPTER SIX:
WELCOME TO THE FUN COLONY

1. "Dante: A Modern Inferno," *Life* (December 17, 1965), p. 38 (six-page foldout).
2. Scott Carpenter, "Scott Carpenter Writes of His Underwater Adventure: 30 Days in Sealab," *Life* (October 15, 1965), p. 100A.
3. Walter Cronkite, "We Are Children of the Space Age," *TV Guide* (July 19, 1969), p. 13.
4. Gordon Cooper, "I've the Normal Desire to Go a Little Higher," *Life* (September 14, 1959), p. 28.
5. John Noble Wilford, *We Reach the Moon* (New York: Bantam Books, 1969), p. 274.
6. Cronkite, "We Are Children of the Space Age," p. 11.

CHAPTER SEVEN: ROBOT LOVE

1. Curt Suplee, "Robot Revolution," *National Geographic* (July 1997), p. 82.
2. Dennis Overbye, "Is Anybody Out There?" *Time* special issue: *Beyond the Year 2000* (Fall 1992), p. 80.
3. Roger G. Gilbertson and John D. Busch, "A Survey of Micro-Actuator Technologies for Future Spacecraft Missions," *Journal of the British Interplanetary Society* (Vol. 49, 1996), pp. 129, 137.

CHAPTER EIGHT: FUTURE TENSE

1. Steven V. Brull, Robert D. Hof, Julia Flynn, and Neil Gross, "Fujitsu Gets Wired," *Business Week* (March 18, 1996), page 1 of article.
2. Fujitsu Interactive, Inc., "Corporate at-a-Glance," corporate statement, 1997.
3. Fujitsu Interactive, Inc., "How Fujitsu Put the 'Art' in 'Artificial Life,'" corporate statement, 1997, pp 2–3.
4. Philip K. Dick, *Time Out of Joint* (reprint, Penguin Books, 1976), p. 159.
5. Fujitsu, "How Fujitsu Put the 'Art' in 'Artificial Life,'" pp. 2–3.
6. Neil Gross, "Into the Wild Frontier," *Business-Week* (June 23, 1997), p. 74.
7. Alvin Toffler, *Future Shock* (New York: Bantam Books, 1972), pp. 449–50.

CHAPTER NINE: THE VIRTUAL REALM

1. Paul Trachtman, "Charles Csuri is an 'Old Master' in a New Medium," *Smithsonian* (February 1995), p. 62.

CHAPTER TEN: POP '97

1. *Chicago Tribune* article as appeared in the *San Francisco Chronicle*, August 19, 1997.

CHAPTER ELEVEN: MESSAGES FROM SPACE

1. Office of Public Affairs, National Aeronautics and Space Administration, *Apollo 8: Man Around the Moon* (Washington, D.C.: U.S. Government Printing Office, 1968), pp. 1, 12.
2. "The Greening of the Astronauts," *Time* (December 11, 1972), p. 43.
3. Ibid.
4. Dr. Edgar Mitchell with Dwight Williams, *The Way of the Explorer* (New York: G. P. Putnam's Sons, 1996), pp. 14–15.
5. Ibid., pp. 58–59.
6. Lincoln Barnett, *The Universe and Dr. Einstein*, revised edition (New York: Bantam Books, 1974), p. 17.
7. Nick Hebert, *Quantum Reality: Beyond the New Physics* (New York: Anchor/Doubleday, 1987), pp. 249–250.
8. David Houston, "Alien Invades Burbank! Thousands Terrified," *Starlog* (May 1980), p. 61.

MARK COTTA VAZ has authored nine books, his first being *Spirit in the Land* (NAL/Signet, 1988), a chronicle of mysticism in the United States. His works on popular culture range from *Tales of the Dark Knight* (Ballantine Books, 1989), the authorized fiftieth birthday celebration of the Batman character, to *Industrial Light & Magic: Into the Digital Realm* (Ballantine Books, 1996), a look at the second decade of the famed effects house. As a board member of the Cartoon Art Museum in San Francisco, he curated the 1992 show "Visions of the Floating World," one of the most comprehensive exhibits ever of original Japanese comics art.

(Author photo by Bruce Walters, XO Digital Arts.)